10 Week-by-Week Sight Word Packets

An Easy System for Teaching 100 Important Sight Words to Set the Stage for Reading Success

Lisa Fitzgerald McKeon

SCHOLASTIC

New York • Toronto • London • Auckland • Sydney
New Delhi • Mexico City • Hong Kong • Buenos Aires

Teaching Resources

Many thanks to all the "little ones" in my life. Just like these "small" sight words, you are powerful beyond measure.

—Lisa

Cover design by Jason Robinson
Interior design by Grafica, Inc.
Illustrations by Susan Stroeher

ISBN: 978-0-545-20458-3

Printed in the U.S.A.

12 13 14 15 16 17 18 19 20 40 24 23 22 21 20 19

Contents

A Note From the Author

For as long as I can remember, the first page of a new book has been full of promise for me. I can recall the excitement I felt as a child each time I walked home from the library, knowing that a newly acquired treasure was safely tucked away in my backpack just waiting to be opened up. It was, in a word, magical. As an adult, things haven't changed much. Books continue to transport me to new places, to new states of mind, and to new experiences. Literacy has been, without a doubt, one of the most powerful tools I have been given in my life.

And so perhaps it is no surprise that I chose literacy as the focus of my adult career. As a Reading Specialist, I assist young children in their acquisition of the deep, well-rooted literacy skills that have served me so well throughout my life. There are, of course, many skills involved in becoming a fluent, accomplished reader. In my professional opinion, one of the first building blocks in this exciting process is to increase a child's sight word vocabulary. The premise is simple—the more words children know, the more able they will be to navigate through a variety of texts and gain meaning from what they have read.

In the pages of this book, I am proud to share the methods and activities I've developed to help young children build up the bank of words they recognize. Time and time again, I've seen children who engage in these activities make great strides in their literacy learning, not only by acquiring the concrete skills they need, but also by developing a love of reading itself. The world of books is indeed a magical one, and I hope this book will help you experience a new kind of magic: the joy that comes from seeing a child discover the endless wonders of the written word.

Enjoy!

Lisa Fitzgerald McKeon

What Are Sight Words and Why Should We Teach Them?

According to educator Robert Hillerich, "Just three words—*I, and, the*—account for ten percent of all words in printed English." Recognizing this, it is easy to see how critical it is that children have a solid grasp of these and other frequently occurring words, for they will be encountering them time and time again in their lives as readers! The activities in this book support young readers by giving them repeated, varied exposure to 100 important sight words. Sight words, also referred to as high-frequency or service words, often cannot be sounded out phonetically. Instead, they need to be recognized "on sight."

Lists of sight words have been around for a long time! In the 1930s after surveying a great quantity of children's books, Edward W. Dolch compiled a list of 220 frequently used words to help parents and educators improve the reading ability of their children. Other commonly used lists include one with 500 words, compiled from the American Heritage Word Frequency Study (Carroll, Davies, and Richman) in the 1970s; and another published by Edward Fry in the 1990s, which incorporates most of the words from the Dolch list, and adds 80 more. *10 Week-by-Week Sight Word Packets* uses the first 100 words from the American Heritage list. However, all of the lists provide excellent starting points for beginning readers.

As readers acquire a larger bank of sight words, over time they are able to quickly and automatically read these words not only in isolation, but also when encountering them in the context of their reading. This automaticity with words, in turn, leads to even greater gains, because as word recognition skills improve, so does comprehension. Why? Because sounding out each and every word takes up time and brain power. The faster children can recognize words, the more time and energy they'll have to devote to understanding the meaning of the words. Comprehending ideas is, of course, the ultimate goal of reading; and learning sight words is an essential step in reaching that goal.

About This Book

10 Week-by-Week Sight Word Packets is the product of my professional research and experience as a reading specialist, and is designed to provide you with a full range of fundamental activities to support emerging and early readers. The activities in each unit systematically introduce and reinforce important sight words and have been used successfully with my own students. Each activity is presented in a simple layout that is both easy to understand and fun to complete, promising to engage even the most reluctant readers.

The book is organized into 10 units of study that together cover 100 high-frequency sight words. Each unit begins with a page that introduces ten new sight words, followed by seven engaging activity sheets that provide children with repeated multisensory exposure to the targeted sight words. The program is flexible, so you can complete the exercises in order, or pick and choose the particular skills or words you'd like to target (see Instructional Options, page 8).

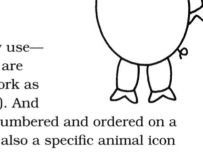

Equally important, the sheets are designed for quick and easy use—just copy a set and you're ready to go! Because the directions are clear and easy to understand, they're ideal for independent work as well as whole-class instruction (see Grouping Options, page 7). And

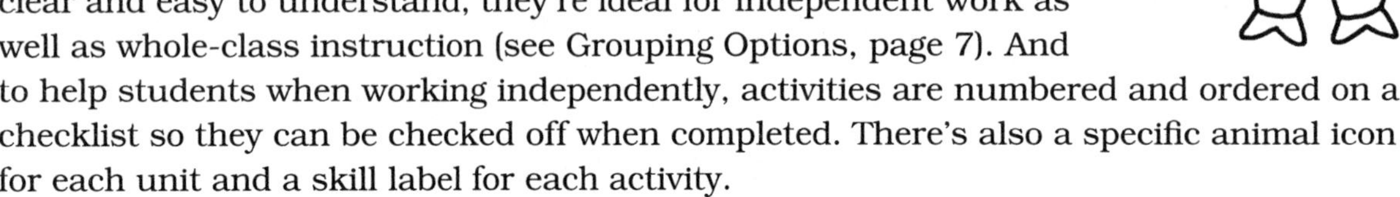

to help students when working independently, activities are numbered and ordered on a checklist so they can be checked off when completed. There's also a specific animal icon for each unit and a skill label for each activity.

About the Activity Skills

Each packet is structured to give children repeated practice with new sight words. The skills involved are designed to address four of the key aspects of language development—reading, speaking, writing, and thinking. Finding activities that focus on a particular skill is a snap; just look for the skill label in the top right-hand corner of each activity page. Following are descriptions of each section and skill, plus tips for leading your learners toward mastery.

- **Introducing:** Children are introduced to ten new sight words in each unit. The first page of the unit allows children to preview the sounds and spellings they will learn in the upcoming activities. The unit openers also act as a tool for self-monitoring. On the right-hand side of the page, children will see a list of all the activity pages in the unit. Encourage children to check off each activity as they complete it.
- **Tracing:** By tracing and copying, children are focusing on the number of letters within each word, left to right directionality, and the order of the letters. They're also building on letter-sound correspondence.
- **Building:** The repetitive nature of systematically building each sight word, letter by letter, helps reinforce spelling skills.
- **Sorting:** Depending on the font style in a book or the handwriting of an adult, not all sight words look the same to early readers! This activity introduces children to a variety of ways that words can be presented in text.
- **Rewriting:** Being able to recognize the configuration of a sight word is an important skill for developing readers. For example, the words *like* and *look* can present as overly similar to early readers as both words begin with *l* and have a *k*. However, aside from the difference in their meanings, there is also a difference in the physical

configuration—or shape—of these words. Early readers need to develop their ability to look at entire words (not just one or two letters) and truly notice such differences. This rewriting activity provides opportunities for children to attend to how words "look" and begin to ask themselves the important question, "Does that look right?"

- **Searching:** Many children enjoy word searches and what better words to look for than the sight words they have been working on? The words in these searches can be found horizontally ⇨ and vertically ⇩ , which helps reinforce the basic print concept of directionality—left to right, top to bottom.
- **Thinking:** Children comprehend text when they gain meaning from written words. In this activity, children get to see and read in context many of the words they've been practicing, and then show their comprehension by matching each sentence with its corresponding illustration. Each sentence contains one or more of the targeted sight words from that unit.
- **Practicing:** To read fluently, one must be able to speak fluently. This activity gives readers the opportunity to practice reading newly acquired sight words aloud. Children practice reading a word list using a variety of voices with the goal of reading each word automatically, smoothly, and fluently. This activity also invites family members to get involved, reinforcing the crucial school-home connection.

Using the Lessons: Helpful Tips

10 Week-by-Week Sight Word Packets is designed for maximum flexibility, so you can easily fit the activities into your curriculum and schedule and tailor them to meet the individual needs of your classroom and students. Following are a few suggestions for making the program a perfect fit for your instructional needs.

Grouping Options

- **Independent Work:** You'll find that the activities in this book are not only lots of fun but also easy for children to understand and complete on their own. You may want to model and review each type of activity throughout the first couple of units; but since the same engaging activity formats are repeated throughout the book, children will likely be able to continue their sight-word learning independently.
- **Partner Work:** Working with a partner can be beneficial for both struggling and advanced readers. When children at different levels work together, the less advanced reader gets support, while the more advanced reader gets the chance to articulate (and therefore reinforce) his or her thinking and problem-solving skills.
- **Small-Group Work:** Working collaboratively helps children gain a variety of skills, as they see how different students approach the same task. Of course, it's also terrific for building social skills!
- **Whole-Class Instruction:** The activities also lend themselves wonderfully to whole-group instruction. You might consider copying an activity sheet onto chart paper so you can lead the class through the activity as children work with their individual copies. Another option is to scan them to use with an interactive whiteboard.

Instructional Options

- **Complete Program:** You can lead children through the program unit by unit throughout the year, going at a pace that suits your schedule and children's skill level. You may choose to do one unit a week or use another time frame. You may decide to spend more time on some units than on others, or to leave out certain units or activities if you've covered those sight words in another part of your curriculum. There are no hard-and-fast rules—the schedule is all up to you!
- **Target Specific Sight Words:** You may find that children have mastered some sight words, but have trouble achieving automaticity with others. Simply select the activities that cover the specific words children need to practice.
- **Use as Homework Packets**: You can send the activity sheets home with children to do as independent homework assignments and to foster the school-home connection. Simply send a note home along with the selected activities, explaining what children are learning with the exercises and encouraging parents and caregivers to work with children on the skills they're developing.

Additional Teaching Supports

- **Reproducible Flashcards:** For your convenience and to support student learning, this book includes a complete set of reproducible flashcards for all 100 targeted sight words.
- **Assessment Checklist:** To help you track progress over time and support the instructional needs of all your learners, reproducible Assessment Checklists are provided for all 100 sight words and are conveniently organized by lesson units.

Connections to the Common Core State Standards

The activities in this book are designed to support you in meeting the following standards in Foundational Skills for Reading for students in grades K–2 outlined in the Common Core State Standards (CCSS). For more information, visit www.corestandards.org.

PHONICS AND WORD RECOGNITION

RF.K.3, RF.1.3, RF.2.3. Know and apply grade-level phonics and word analysis skills in decoding words.

RF.K.3c. Read common high-frequency words by sight (e.g., *the, of, to, you, she, my, is, are, do, does*).

RF.1.3g, RF.2.3f. Recognize and read grade-appropriate irregularly spelled words.

FLUENCY

RF.K.4. Read emergent-reader texts with purpose and understanding.

RF.1.4, RF.2.4. Read with sufficient accuracy and fluency to support comprehension.

RF.1.4a, RF.2.4a. Read grade-level text with purpose and understanding.

RF.1.4c, RF.2.4c. Use context to confirm or self-correct word recognition and understanding, rereading as necessary.

Name ______________________________

Sight Word Packet 1

the

of

and

a

to

in

is

you

that

it

✔ off each activity after you complete it.

- ❑ Activity 1: **Tracing**
- ❑ Activity 2: **Building**
- ❑ Activity 3: **Sorting**
- ❑ Activity 4: **Rewriting**
- ❑ Activity 5: **Searching**
- ❑ Activity 6: **Thinking**
- ❑ Activity 7: **Practicing**

 Name ______________________

Take a Good Look!

Trace each sight word. Then copy it on the lines to fill in the glasses.

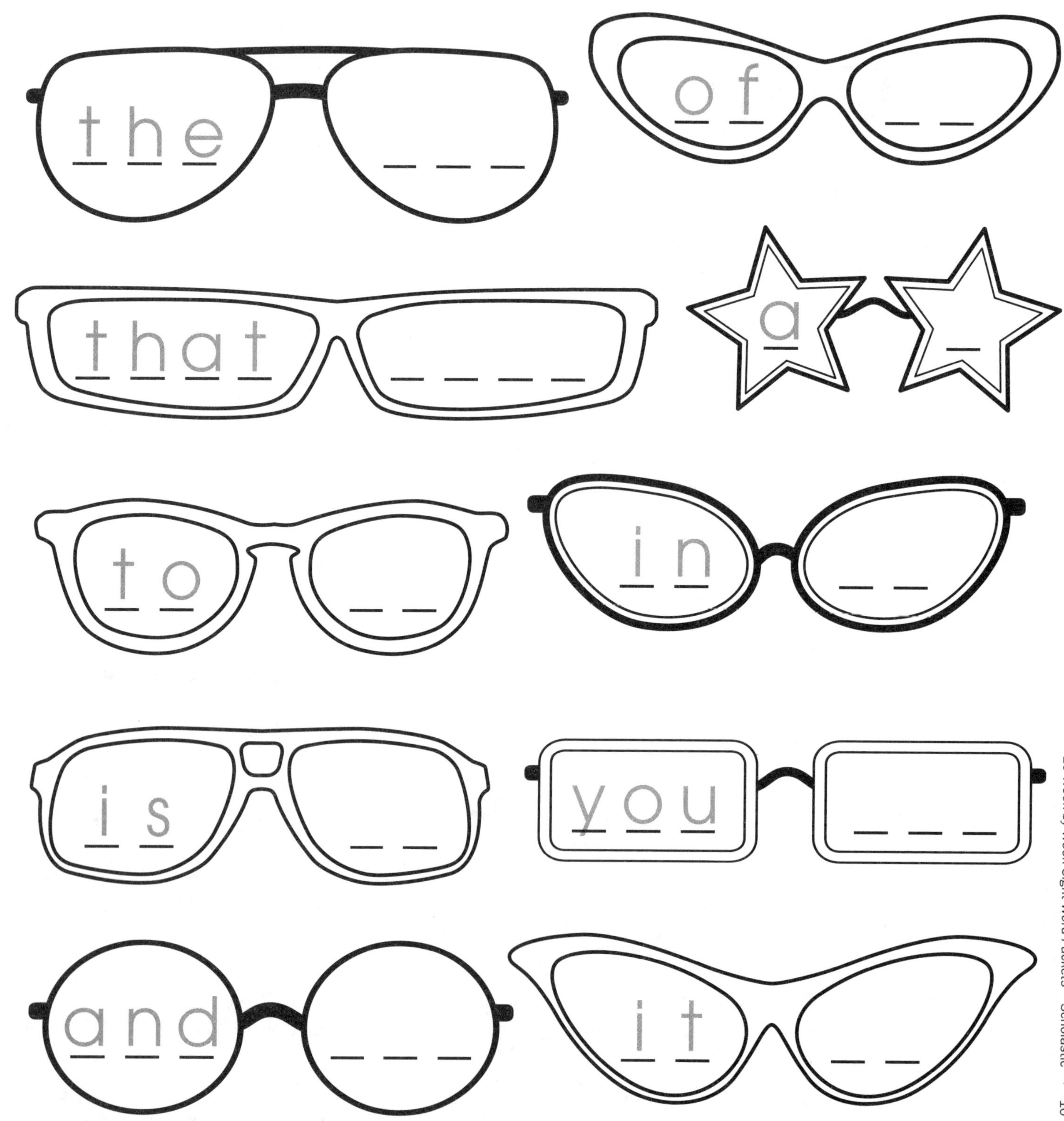

Sight Word Packet 1 Name ______________________

Activity 2

Building

One Letter at a Time

Fill in the letters one at a time to build a word pyramid. One has been done for you.

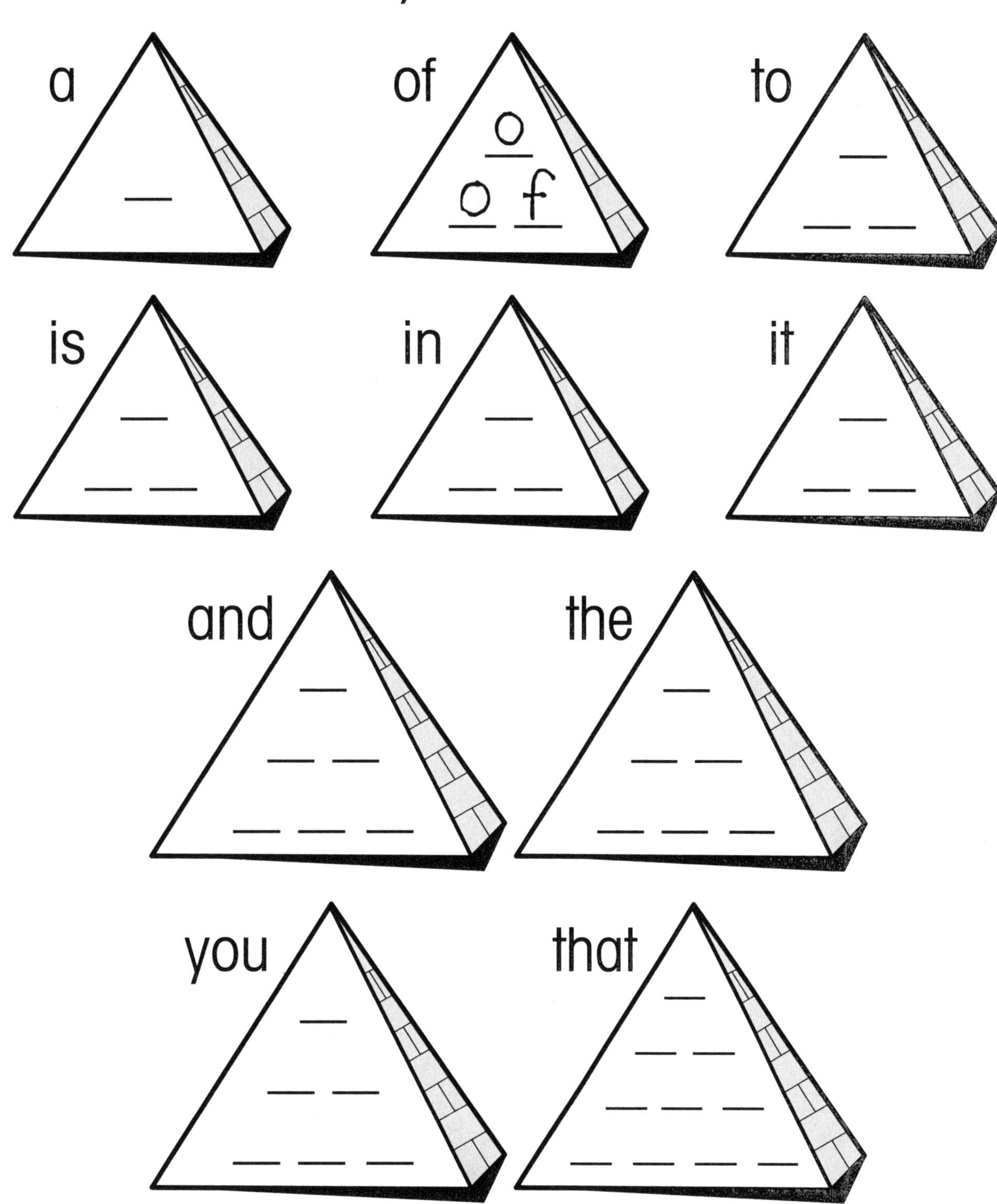

Name ______________________________

Towering Word Sets

Draw lines from tower to tower to match each set of words.

the	it
of	of
that	is
a	you
to	and
in	that
is	a
you	the
and	to
it	in

Name ______________________

Get in Shape!

Write each word in the shape box that fits.
One has been done for you.

the	~~of~~	that	a	to
in	is	you	and	it

o f

Name ______________________________

Hide and Seek Word Search

Use a pencil and circle the words from the list below.
Look for words going across ⇨ and down ⇩.
The first one has been done for you.

~~THE~~	TO	YOU
OF	IN	THAT
AND	IS	IT

Y	J	G	S	J	B	R	A	W	Z
B	T	T	H	E	I	U	C	L	T
C	O	P	C	O	X	Y	D	B	H
M	I	S	E	S	N	O	A	V	A
I	S	K	Z	M	L	U	Z	C	T
E	O	O	F	G	P	A	R	O	N
I	K	M	F	C	O	N	K	S	X
T	V	S	Y	J	D	D	N	R	I
P	E	C	C	O	Z	Y	D	Z	B
D	E	H	D	M	F	I	N	D	E

Name ______________________________

Picture It!

Read each sentence and look at the pictures. Draw a line to connect each picture to the sentence it goes with.

You go to school.

That is a toy.

The boy is sad and mad.

It is in the car.

The house is made of wood.

Name ______________________________

Activity 7

Practicing

Listen to Me!

Have fun reading each word aloud to your family using the different voices. Be sure to get your paper signed and return it to school.

the

of

and

to

in

is

a

you

that

it

Read these words using a SCARY voice.

Read these words using a silly voice.

Read these words using a whisper voice.

Read these words using a teacher voice.

Read these words using a ROBOT voice.

______________________ read _____ out of 10 words quickly and accurately.

______________________________________ Parent/Guardian Signature

Name ______________________________

he
for
was
on
are
as
with
his
they
at

✔ off each activity after you complete it.

- ❑ Activity 1: **Tracing**
- ❑ Activity 2: **Building**
- ❑ Activity 3: **Sorting**
- ❑ Activity 4: **Rewriting**
- ❑ Activity 5: **Searching**
- ❑ Activity 6: **Thinking**
- ❑ Activity 7: **Practicing**

Name ______________________

Activity 1

Tracing

Take a Good Look!

Trace each sight word. Then copy it on the lines to fill in the glasses.

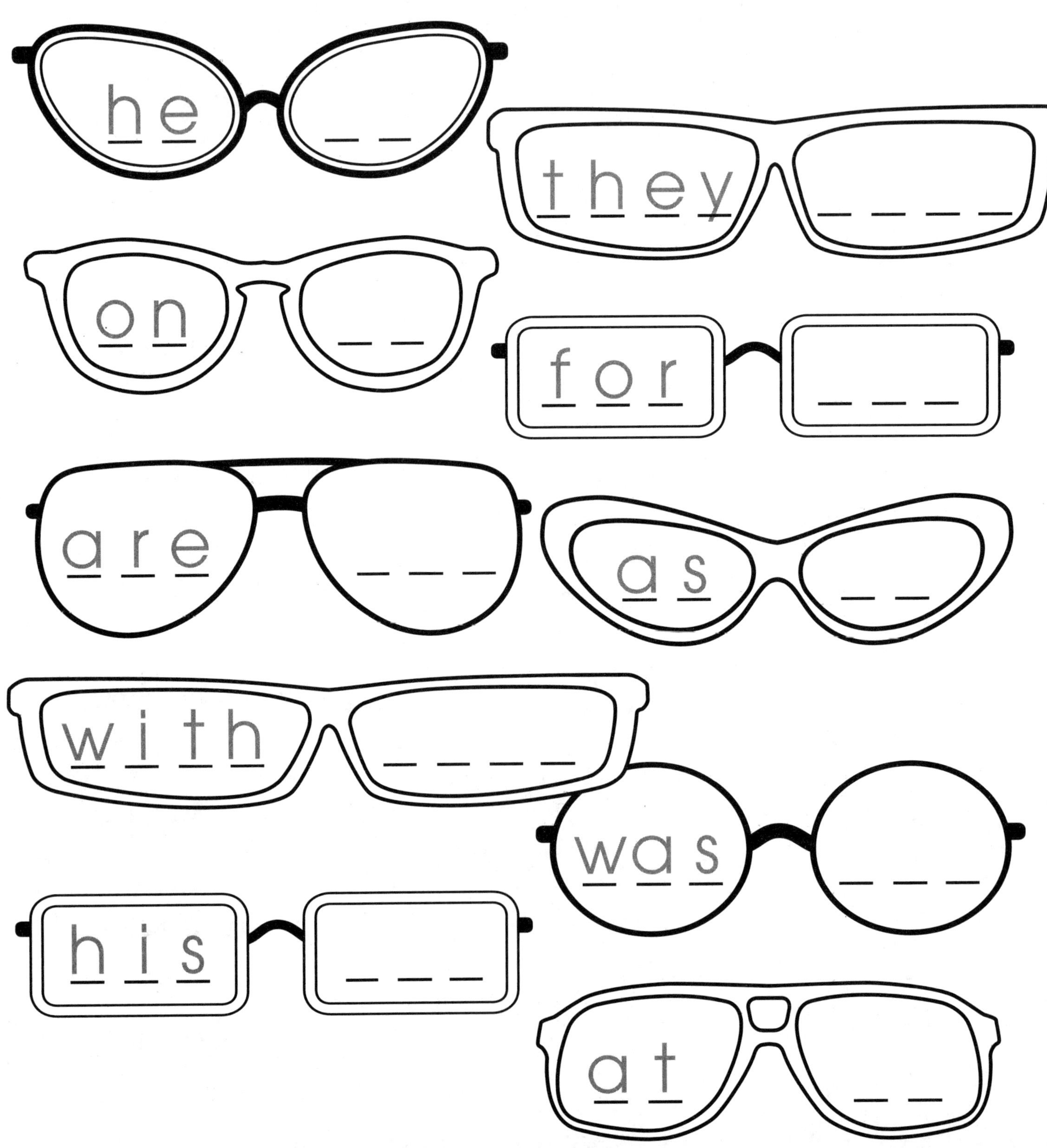

Name ___________________________

One Letter at a Time

Fill in the letters one at a time to build a word pyramid. The first one has been done for you.

he

for

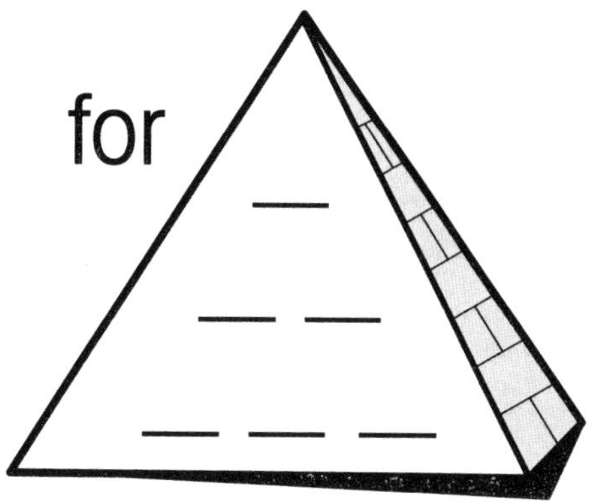

was

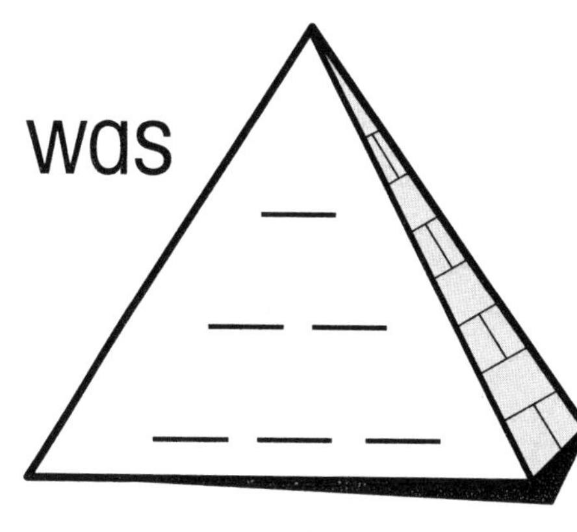

on

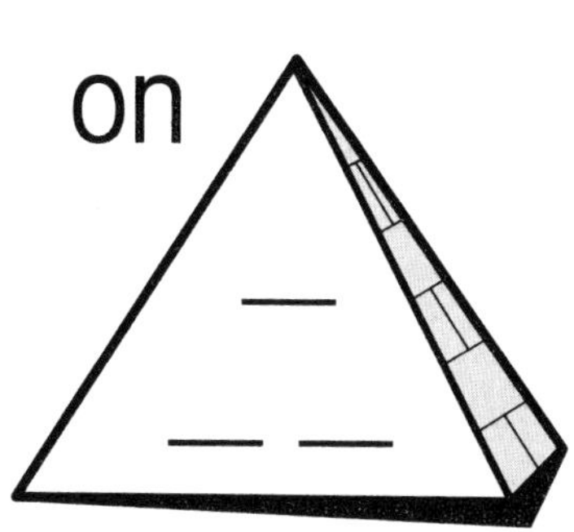

are

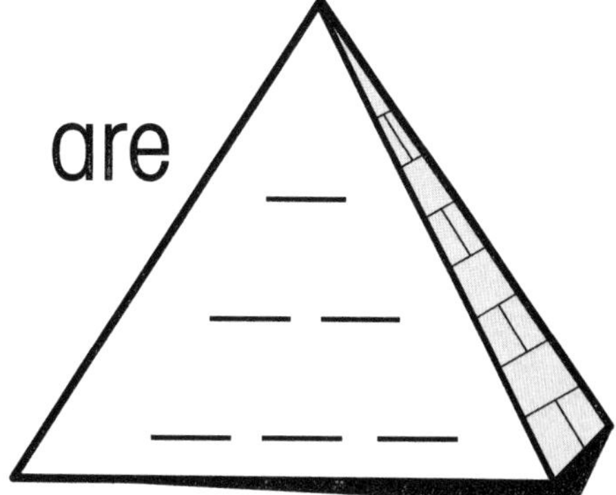

his

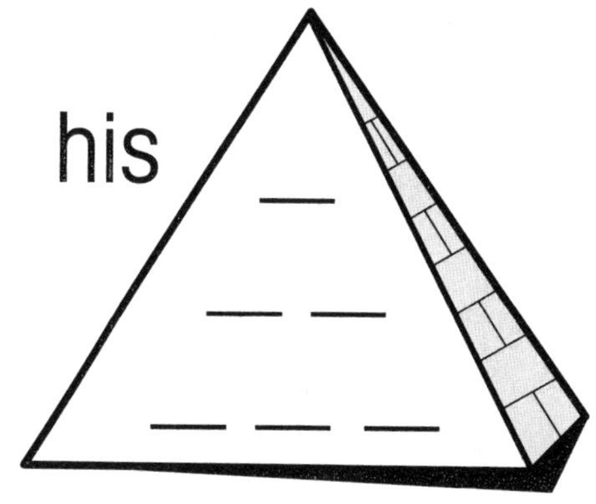

as

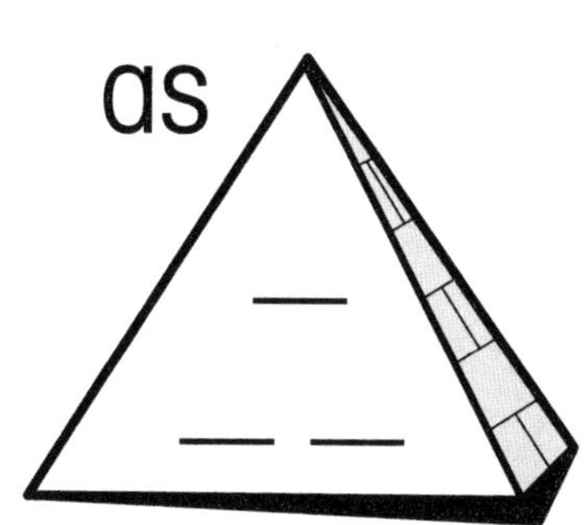

with

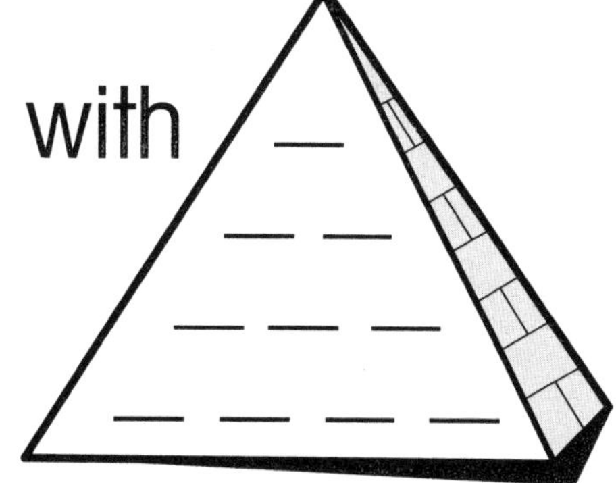

they

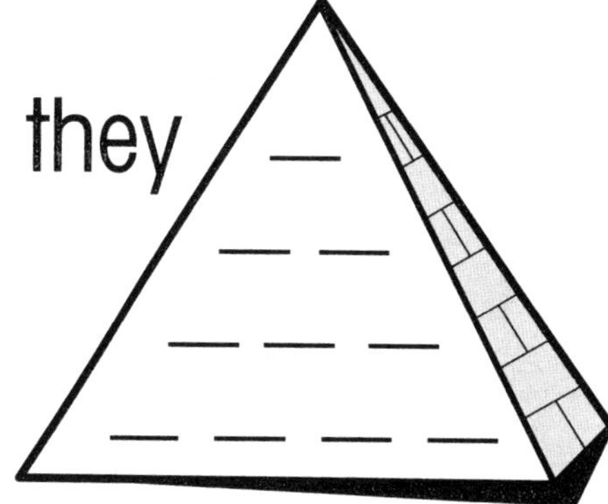

at

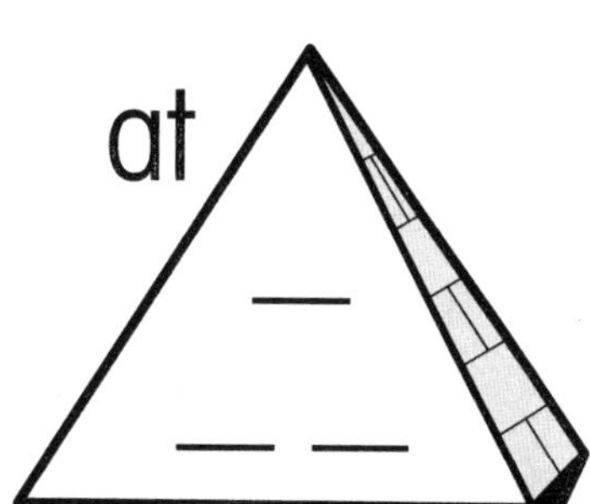

Name ______________________

Activity 3

Sorting

Towering Word Sets

Draw lines from tower to tower to match each set of words.

he	at
for	for
was	with
on	he
are	his
as	they
with	was
his	on
they	are
at	as

Name ______________________________

Get in Shape!

Write each word in the shape box that fits.
One has been done for you.

he	for	was	~~on~~	are
as	with	his	they	at

on

Name ______________________________

Hide and Seek Word Search

Use a pencil and circle the words from the list below.
Look for words going across ⇨ and down ⇩.
The first one has been done for you.

~~HE~~	WAS	ARE	WITH	THEY
FOR	ON	AS	HIS	AT

S	J	Y	Q	Z	T	M	X	U	B
R	M	F	O	R	B	J	A	R	E
H	H	P	M	D	F	C	Y	A	O
I	Y	N	K	X	L	A	X	S	N
S	W	W	A	S	I	E	N	D	R
K	W	I	T	H	H	R	U	I	L
T	H	E	Y	B	A	B	L	I	C
D	A	T	H	G	A	M	E	V	C
(H	E)	T	H	R	S	C	U	B	H
I	H	X	Q	V	Q	Y	D	R	A

Name ___________________________________

Picture It!

Read each sentence and look at the pictures. Draw a line to connect each picture to the sentence it goes with.

He was on the soccer team.

They are with his mom.

That dog is as big as me!

They are at the park for a birthday party.

The pool is for swimming.

Sight Word Packet 2 Name ______________________________

Activity 7

Practicing

Listen to Me!

Have fun reading each word aloud to your family using the different voices. Be sure to get your paper signed and return it to school.

he

at

for

they

was

his

on

with

are

as

Read these words using a SCARY voice.

Read these words using a silly voice.

Read these words using a whisper voice.

Read these words using a teacher voice.

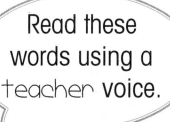

Read these words using a ROBOT voice.

______________________ read _____ out of 10 words quickly and accurately.

______________________________________ Parent/Guardian Signature

Name ______________________________

be	this
from	I
have	or
by	one
had	not

✔ off each activity after you complete it.

- ❑ Activity 1: **Tracing**
- ❑ Activity 2: **Building**
- ❑ Activity 3: **Sorting**
- ❑ Activity 4: **Rewriting**
- ❑ Activity 5: **Searching**
- ❑ Activity 6: **Thinking**
- ❑ Activity 7: **Practicing**

Name ____________________

Activity 1
Tracing

Take a Good Look!

Trace each sight word. Then copy it on the lines to fill in the glasses.

Name ___________________________

One Letter at a Time

Fill in the letters one at a time to build a word pyramid. One has been done for you.

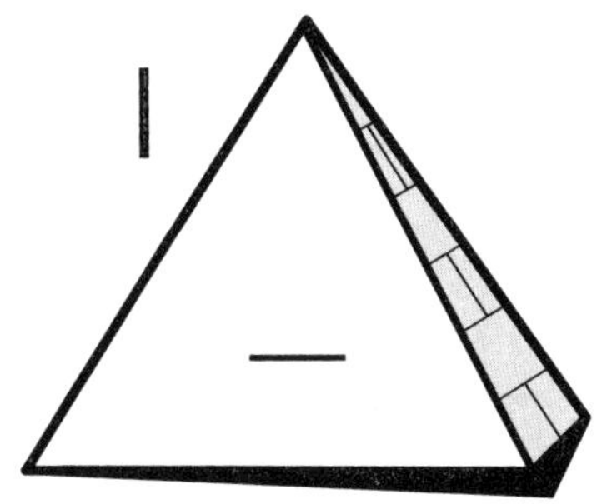

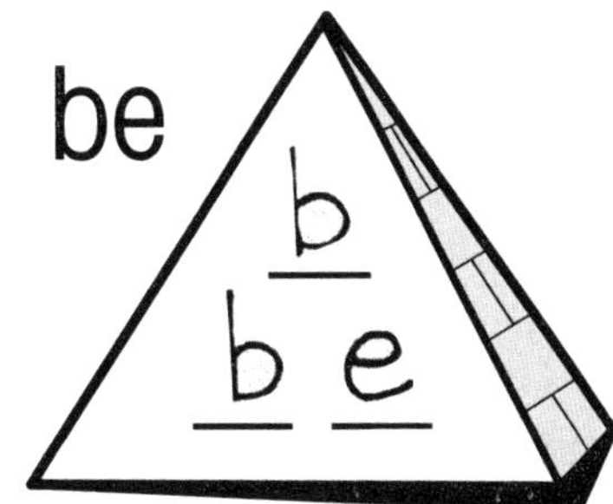

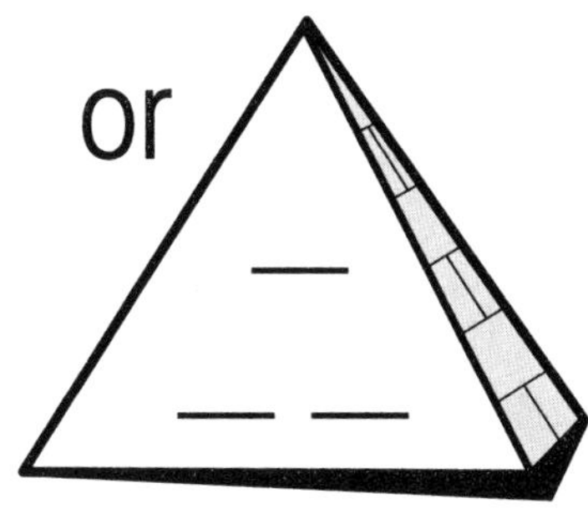

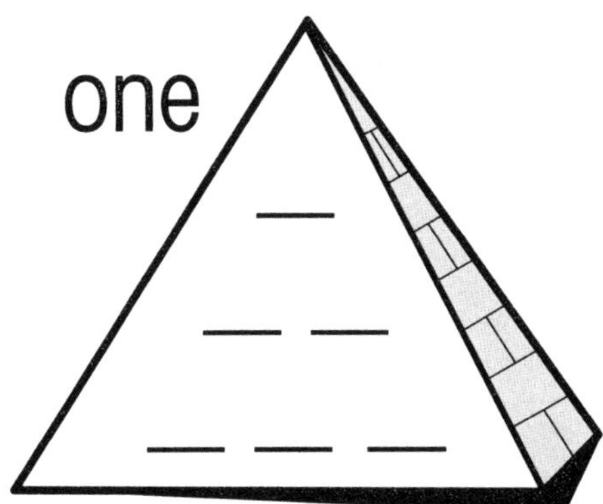

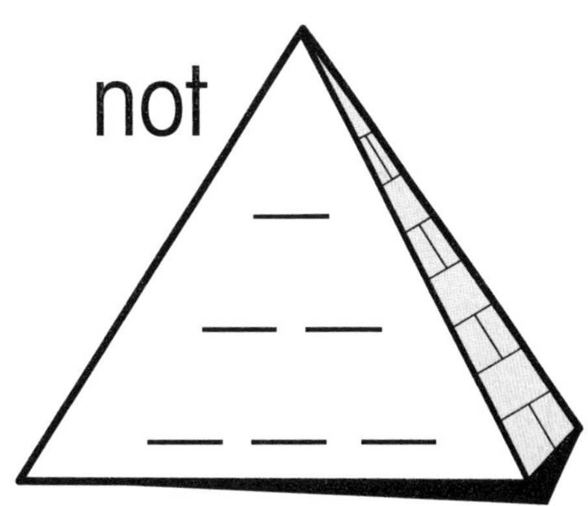

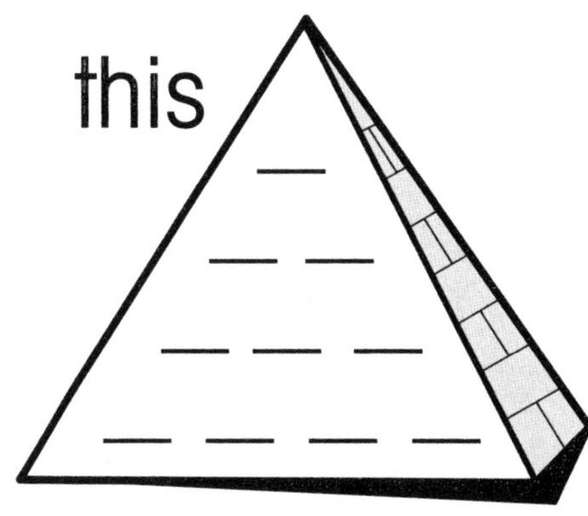

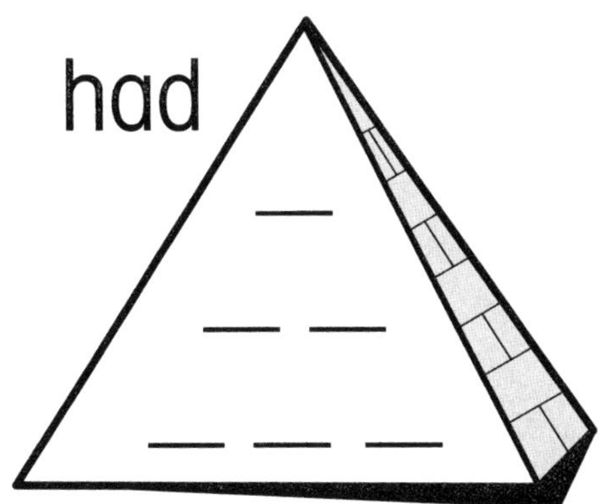

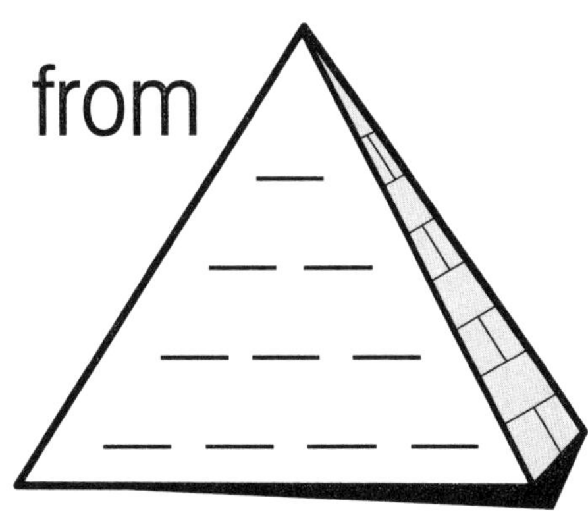

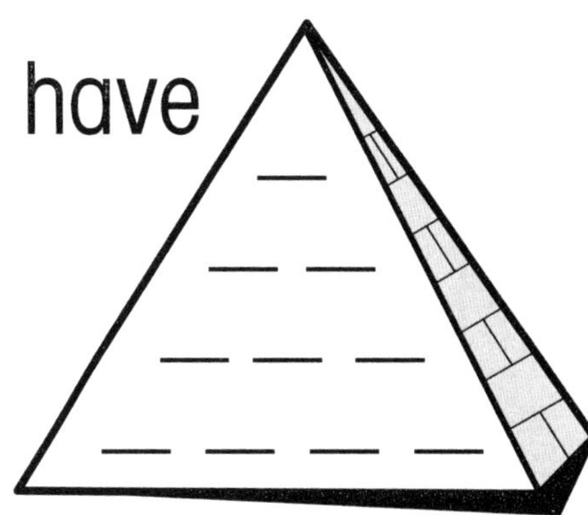

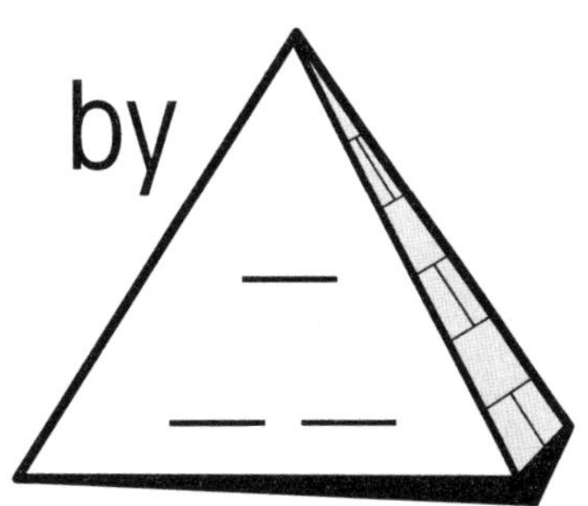

 Name ______________________

Towering Word Sets

Draw lines from tower to tower to match each set of words.

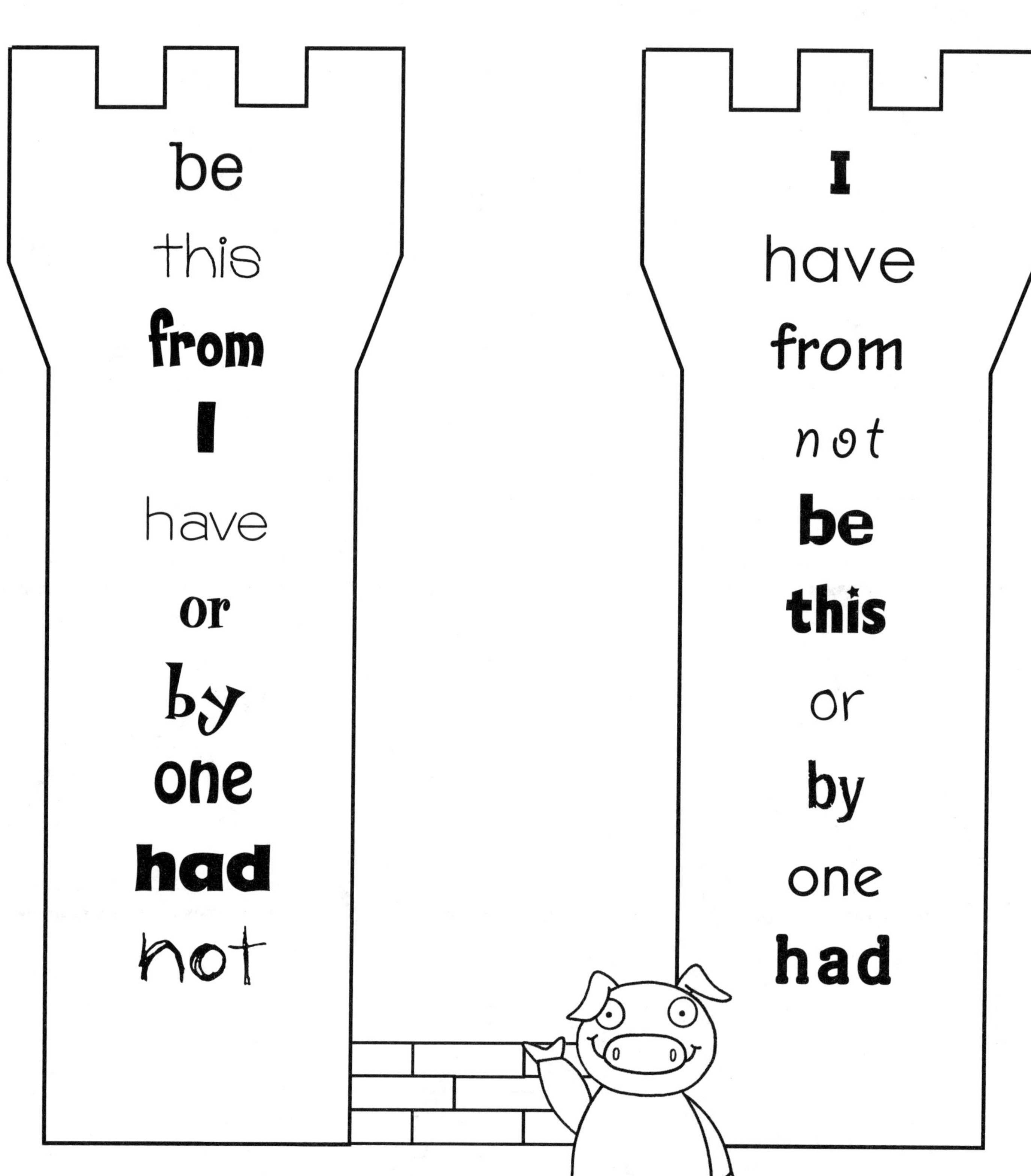

Name ______________________________

Get in Shape!

Write each word in the shape box that fits.
The first one has been done for you.

~~be~~	this	from	I	have
or	by	one	had	not

be

Sight Word Packet 3 Name ____________________

Hide and Seek Word Search

Use a pencil and circle the words from the list below.
Look for words going across ⇨ and down ⇩.
The first one has been done for you.

~~BE~~	HAVE	ONE
THIS	OR	HAD
FROM	BY	NOT

B J P Y N Q L B R F
J G F R O M U R D N
I B D X T D I X T F
Q T G Z Z C C I S M
V B Y A G P Q K O B
A D C X R I J U R M
O T H I S X L Y D B
N S A H A V E G N E
E V D E R V H N G V
S T Y U M F Q J Q D

 Name ______________________________

Activity 6

Thinking

Picture It!

Read each sentence and look at the pictures. Draw a line to connect each picture to the sentence it goes with.

I have one fish.

He was not in school or at home.

This is from my house by the beach.

I had milk and one cookie.

They have to be brother and sister.

Sight Word Packet 3 Name ____________________

Listen to Me!

Have fun reading each word aloud to your family using the different voices. Be sure to get your paper signed and return it to school.

be

not

this

had

from

one

I

by

have

or

Read these words using a SCARY voice.
Read these words using a silly voice.
Read these words using a whisper voice.
Read these words using a teacher voice.
Read these words using a ROBOT voice.

____________________ read _____ out of 10 words quickly and accurately.

____________________ Parent/Guardian Signature

Name ______________________________

but	what
all	were
we	when
an	can
there	your

✔ off each activity after you complete it.

- ❑ Activity 1: **Tracing**
- ❑ Activity 2: **Building**
- ❑ Activity 3: **Sorting**
- ❑ Activity 4: **Rewriting**
- ❑ Activity 5: **Searching**
- ❑ Activity 6: **Thinking**
- ❑ Activity 7: **Practicing**

Name ________________________________

Take a Good Look!

Trace each sight word. Then copy it on the lines to fill in the glasses.

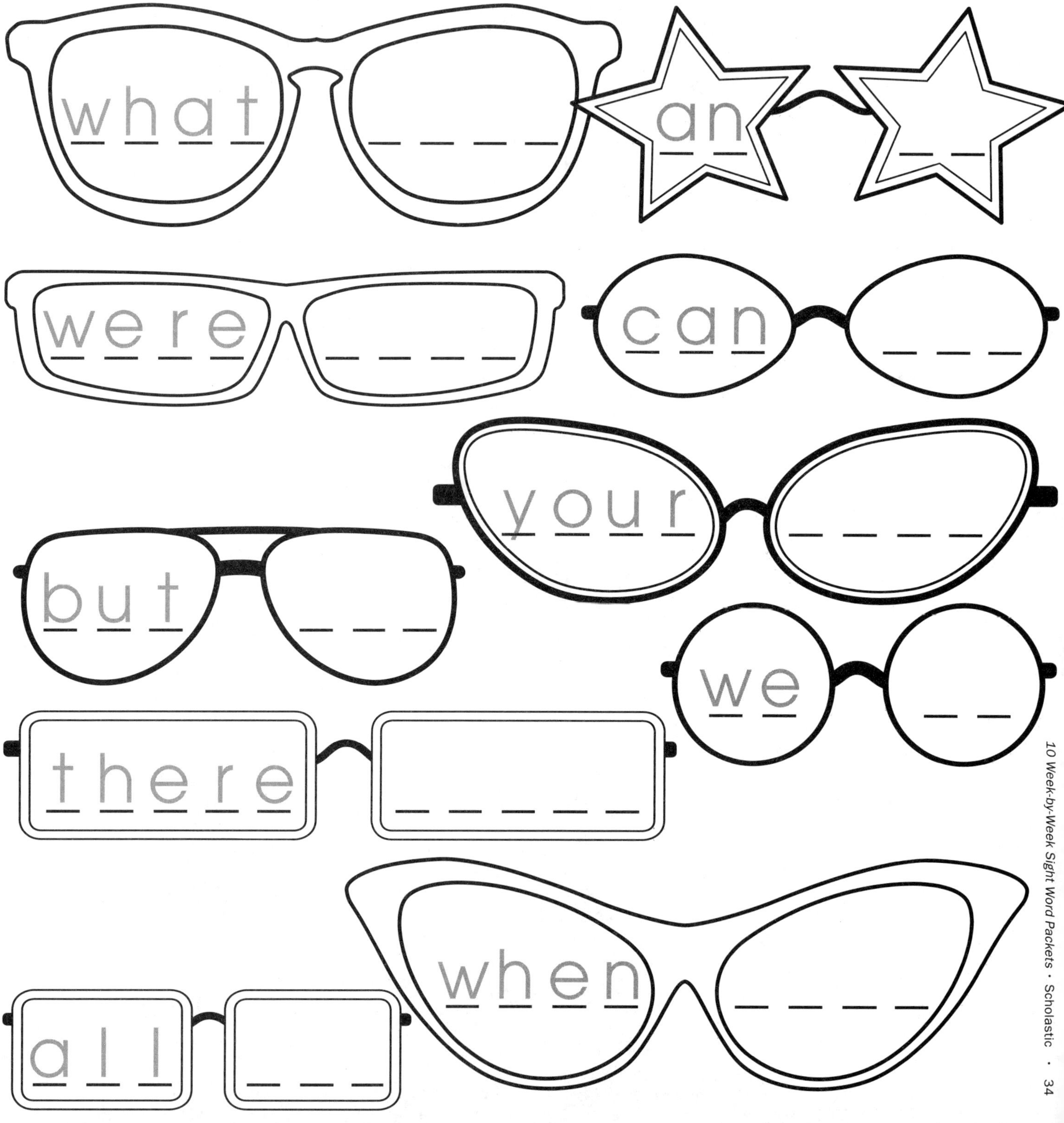

what ____

an __

were ____

can ___

your ____

but ___

we __

there _____

when ____

all ___

Sight Word Packet 4 Name ________________________________

One Letter at a Time

Fill in the letters one at a time to build a word pyramid. The first one has been done for you.

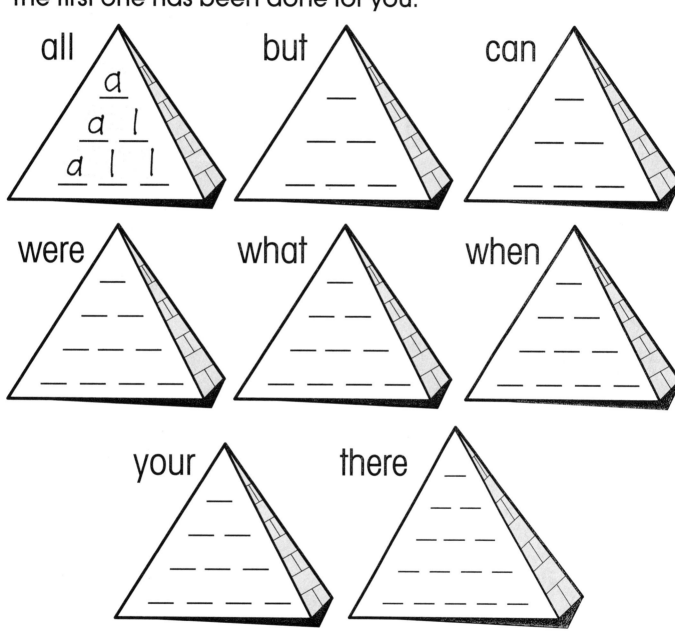

all

a

a l

a l l

but

can

were

what

when

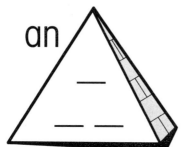

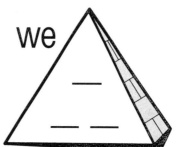

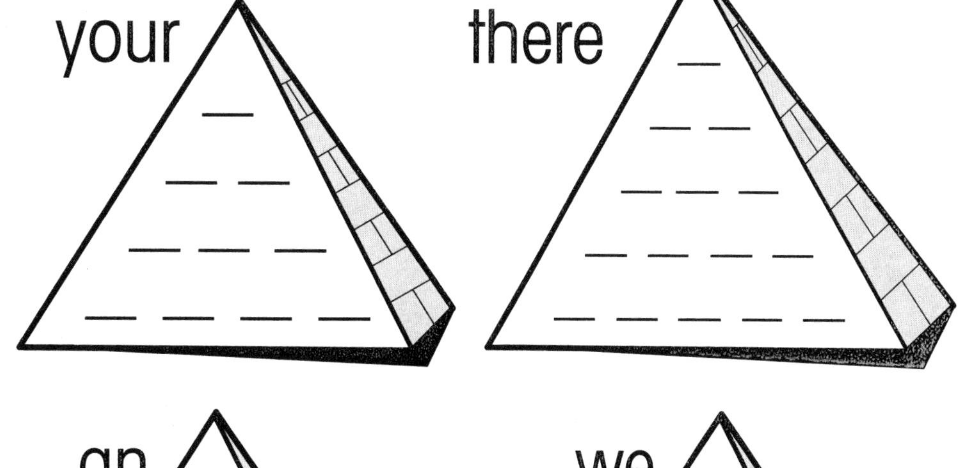

an

we

Name ______________________________

Towering Word Sets

Draw lines from tower to tower to match each set of words.

but	all
what	an
all	YOUR
were	when
when	but
we	were
there	what
can	we
an	there
your	can

Name ______________________________

Get in Shape!

Write each word in the shape box that fits.
One has been done for you.

but	what	all	were	when
~~we~~	there	can	an	your

we

 Name ______________________________

Hide and Seek Word Search

Use a pencil and circle the words from the list below. Look for words going across ⇨ and down ⇩. The first one has been done for you.

~~BUT~~	ALL	WHEN	THERE	AN
WHAT	WERE	WE	CAN	YOUR

R	S	V	F	H	E	G	J	S	D
Q	Q	T	A	Y	O	H	U	L	G
N	O	T	Y	O	U	R	W	P	I
S	K	W	Y	W	K	B	Z	J	D
F	N	E	Q	J	S	T	A	C	S
U	E	R	A	B	E	H	H	E	Z
W	H	E	N	U	Q	E	C	A	N
M	W	H	A	T	B	R	L	L	S
A	P	V	L	Y	T	E	F	L	X
Q	Z	X	A	O	F	K	L	W	E

 Name ______________________________

Picture It!

Read each sentence and look at the pictures. Draw a line to connect each picture to the sentence it goes with.

Can I have an apple?

When did we go there?

What is your name?

We were all in the car.

I have my bag, but forgot my hat.

 Name ______________________________

Listen to Me!

Have fun reading each word aloud to your family using the different voices. Be sure to get your paper signed and return it to school.

but
your
what
an
all
can
were
there
when
we

Read these words using a SCARY voice.

Read these words using a silly voice.

Read these words using a whisper voice.

Read these words using a teacher voice.

Read these words using a ROBOT voice.

______________________ read _____ out of 10 words quickly and accurately.

______________________________________ Parent/Guardian Signature

Name ___________________________

which if

their said

will do

about each

how up

✔ off each activity after you complete it.

- ❑ Activity 1: **Tracing**
- ❑ Activity 2: **Building**
- ❑ Activity 3: **Sorting**
- ❑ Activity 4: **Rewriting**
- ❑ Activity 5: **Searching**
- ❑ Activity 6: **Thinking**
- ❑ Activity 7: **Practicing**

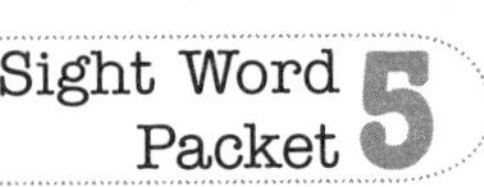

Name ____________________

Take a Good Look!

Trace each sight word. Then copy it on the lines to fill in the glasses.

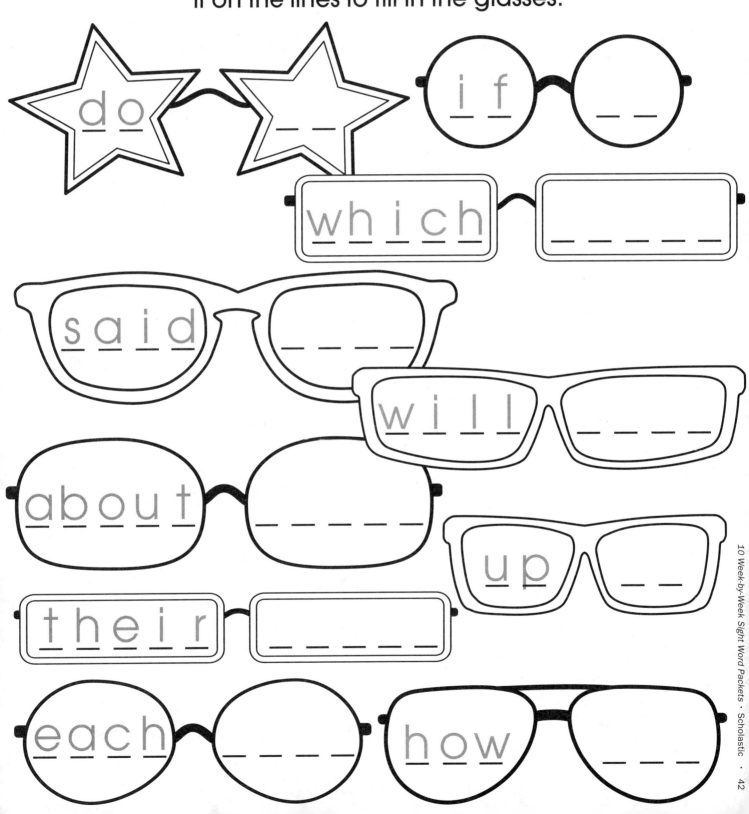

do __ __

if __ __

which __ __ __ __ __

said __ __ __ __

will __ __ __ __

about __ __ __ __ __

up __ __

their __ __ __ __ __

each __ __ __ __

how __ __ __

Sight Word Packet 5 Name ____________________

One Letter at a Time

Fill in the letters one at a time to build a word pyramid.
One has been done for you.

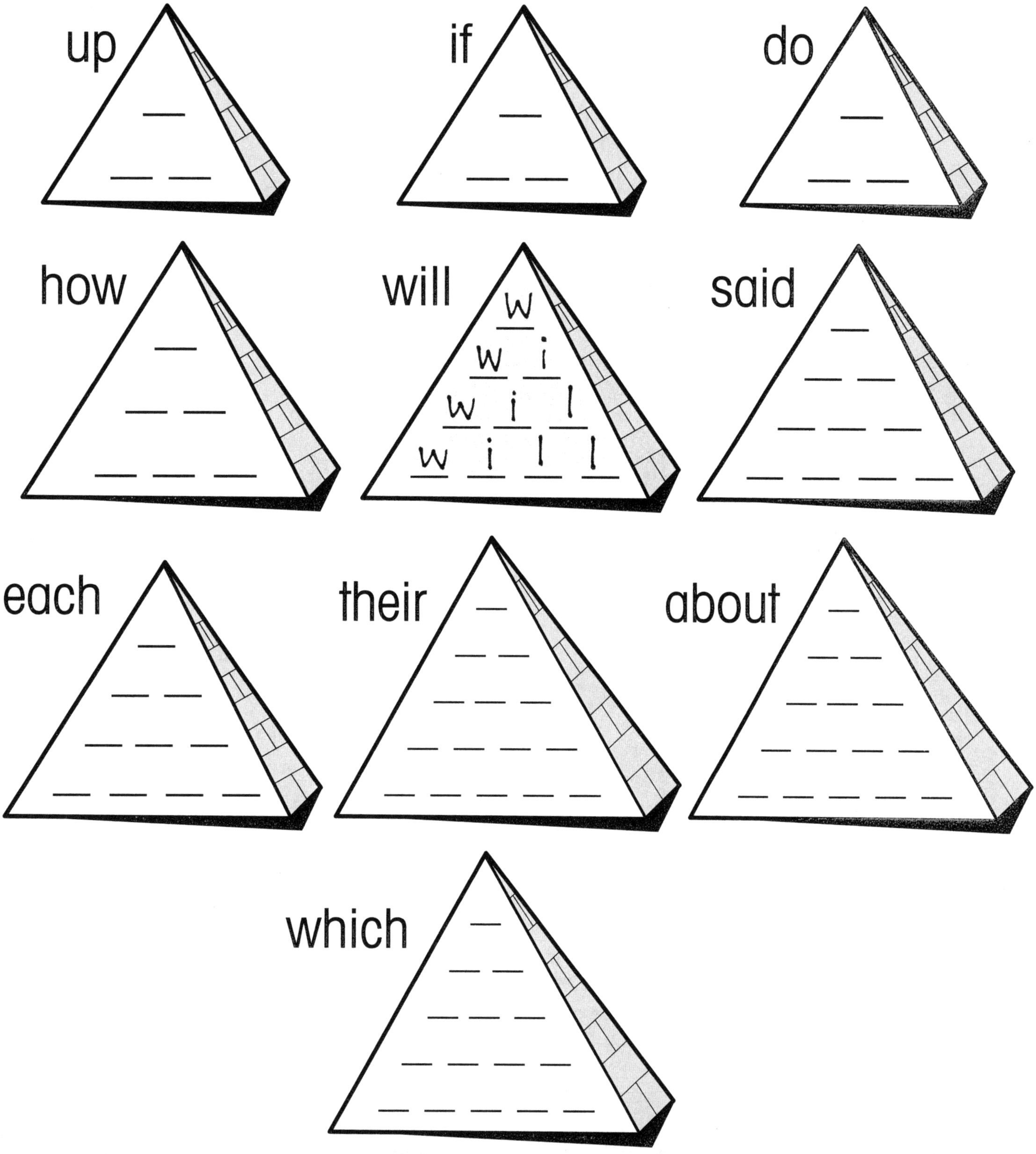

up

if

do

how

will

w
w i
w i l
w i l l

said

each

their

about

which

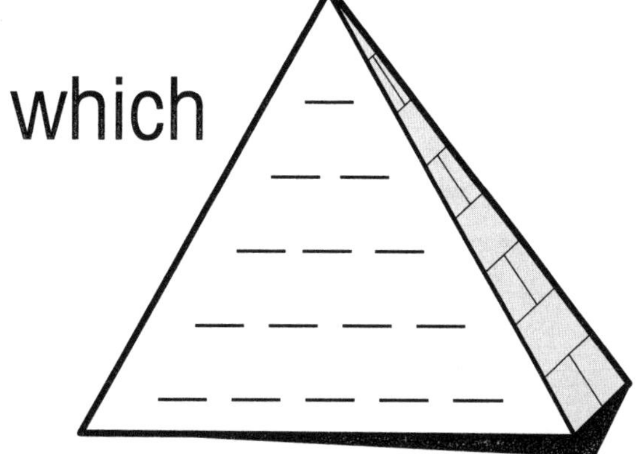

Name ________________________________

Towering Word Sets

Draw lines from tower to tower to match each set of words.

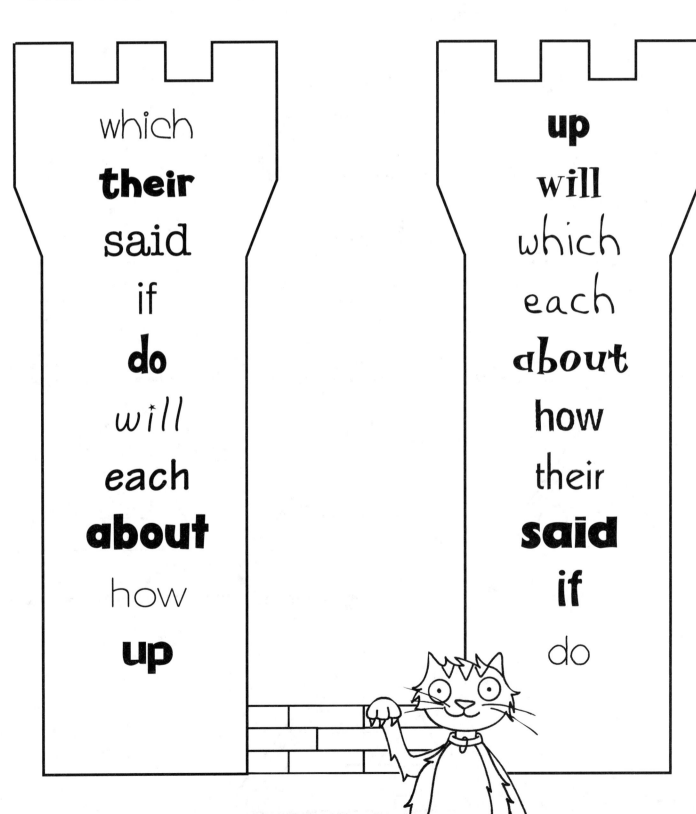

which	up
their	will
said	which
if	each
do	about
will	how
each	their
about	said
how	if
up	do

Name ______________________________

Get in Shape!

Write each word in the shape box that fits.
One has been done for you.

which	their	said	~~if~~	do
will	each	about	how	up

i f

 Name ______________________________

Hide and Seek Word Search

Use a pencil and circle the words from the list below.
Look for words going across ⇨ and down ⇩.
The first one has been done for you.

~~SAID~~	THEIR	DO	EACH	HOW
WHICH	IF	WILL	ABOUT	UP

N	S	A	I	D	E	K	X	R	W
W	H	H	N	C	A	D	Y	X	E
H	G	C	P	A	B	O	U	T	A
I	U	D	T	H	E	I	R	L	C
C	U	P	W	B	H	F	E	H	H
H	O	W	S	W	W	J	U	U	N
S	B	J	N	I	Q	A	W	S	V
T	F	N	X	L	H	U	F	C	H
U	A	B	B	L	X	W	F	S	T
U	L	J	I	T	I	R	G	E	O

 Name ______________________________

Picture It!

Read each sentence and look at the pictures. Draw a line to connect each picture to the sentence it goes with.

How about we get an ice cream?

Their kite is up in the sky.

If I do my homework now, I can watch TV after dinner.

Which dress do you like?

We will each have a piece of cake.

Name ______________________________

Practicing

Listen to Me!

Have fun reading each word aloud to your family using the different voices. Be sure to get your paper signed and return it to school.

which

up

their

how

said

about

if

each

do

will

Read these words using a SCARY voice.

Read these words using a silly voice.

Read these words using a whisper voice.

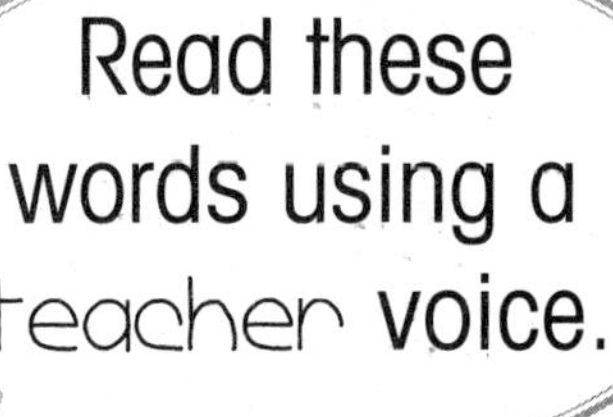

Read these words using a teacher voice.

Read these words using a ROBOT voice.

______________________ read _____ out of 10 words quickly and accurately.

______________________________ Parent/Guardian Signature

Name ______________________________

them out

then she

many some

so these

would other

✔ off each activity after you complete it.

- ❑ Activity 1: **Tracing**
- ❑ Activity 2: **Building**
- ❑ Activity 3: **Sorting**
- ❑ Activity 4: **Rewriting**
- ❑ Activity 5: **Searching**
- ❑ Activity 6: **Thinking**
- ❑ Activity 7: **Practicing**

Sight Word Packet 6 Name ______________________

Take a Good Look!

Trace each sight word. Then copy it on the lines to fill in the glasses.

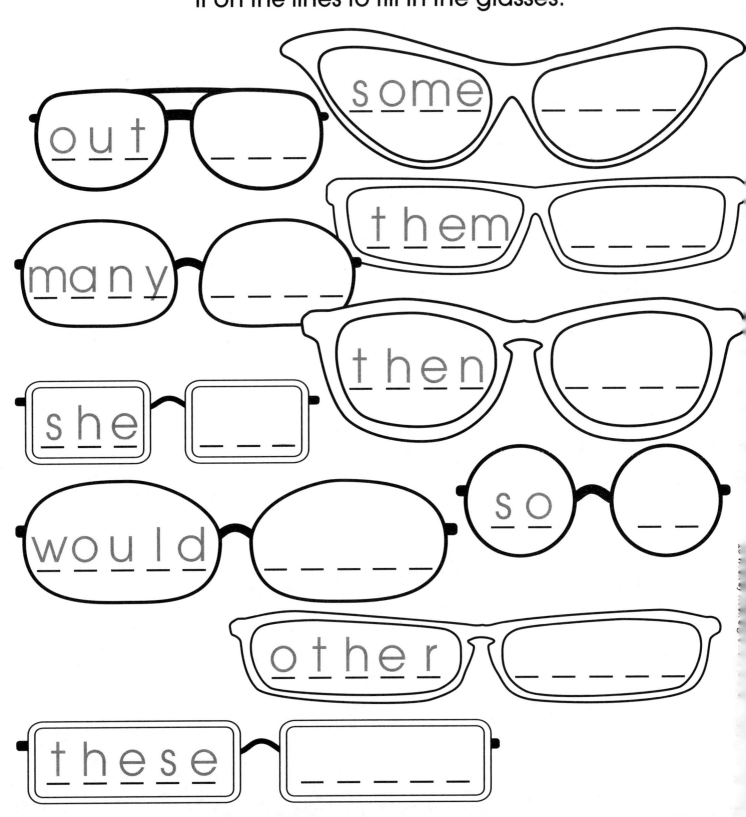

some _ _ _ _

out _ _ _

them _ _ _ _

many _ _ _ _

then _ _ _ _

she _ _ _

so _ _

would _ _ _ _ _

other _ _ _ _ _

these _ _ _ _ _

Name ______________________________

One Letter at a Time

Fill in the letters one at a time to build a word pyramid. The first one has been done for you.

 Name ______________________________

Towering Word Sets

Draw lines from tower to tower to match each set of words.

Name ___________________________

Get in Shape!

Write each word in the shape box that fits.
One has been done for you.

out	them	then	she	many
some	~~so~~	these	would	other

s o

 Name ______________________________

Hide and Seek Word Search

Use a pencil and circle the words from the list below.
Look for words going across ⇨ and down ⇩.
The first one has been done for you.

~~OUT~~	THEN	MANY	SO	WOULD
THEM	SHE	SOME	THESE	OTHER

Q	D	B	M	I	V	J	R	P	M
S	T	H	E	N	W	F	W	G	Y
H	W	C	P	K	I	E	F	J	D
E	O	T	H	E	R	M	G	J	S
X	U	W	C	C	X	D	X	F	O
D	L	M	W	M	R	T	H	E	M
M	D	Y	M	G	T	H	E	S	E
Y	R	F	F	L	F	E	L	C	M
Z	M	M	A	N	Y	S	O	T	O
N	O	U	T	E	T	Y	T	E	Y

 Name ____________________

Picture It!

Read each sentence and look at the pictures. Draw a line to connect each picture to the sentence it goes with.

She went out the door of her house.

These flowers would be a nice gift.

Some of them are babies.

She read a book and then went to bed.

There are many other things we can do at the beach.

 Name ____________________

Listen to Me!

Have fun reading each word aloud to your family using the different voices. Be sure to get your paper signed and return it to school.

- out
- other
- them
- would
- then
- these
- she
- so
- many
- some

Read these words using a SCARY voice.

Read these words using a silly voice.

Read these words using a whisper voice.

Read these words using a teacher voice.

Read these words using a ROBOT voice.

____________________ read _____ out of 10 words quickly and accurately.

____________________ Parent/Guardian Signature

Name ______________________________

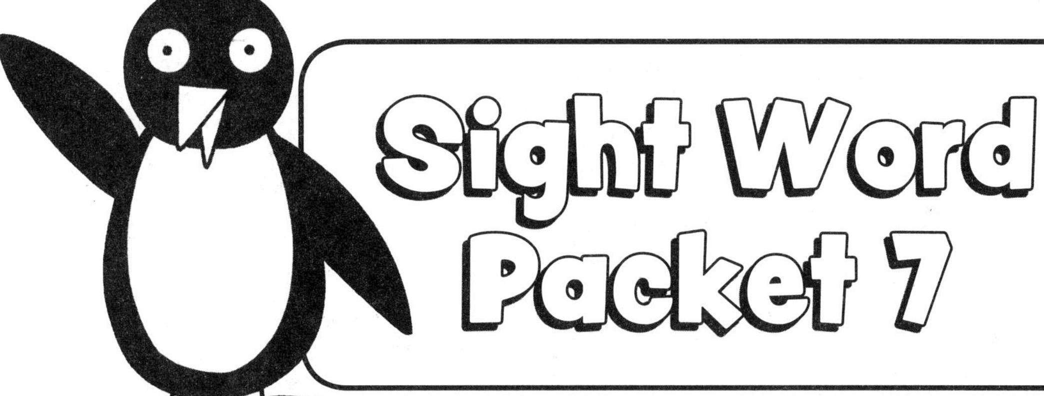

into has

more her

two like

him see

time could

✔ off each activity after you complete it.

❑ Activity 1: **Tracing**

❑ Activity 2: **Building**

❑ Activity 3: **Sorting**

❑ Activity 4: **Rewriting**

❑ Activity 5: **Searching**

❑ Activity 6: **Thinking**

❑ Activity 7: **Practicing**

 Name ____________________

Take a Good Look!

Trace each sight word. Then copy it on the lines to fill in the glasses.

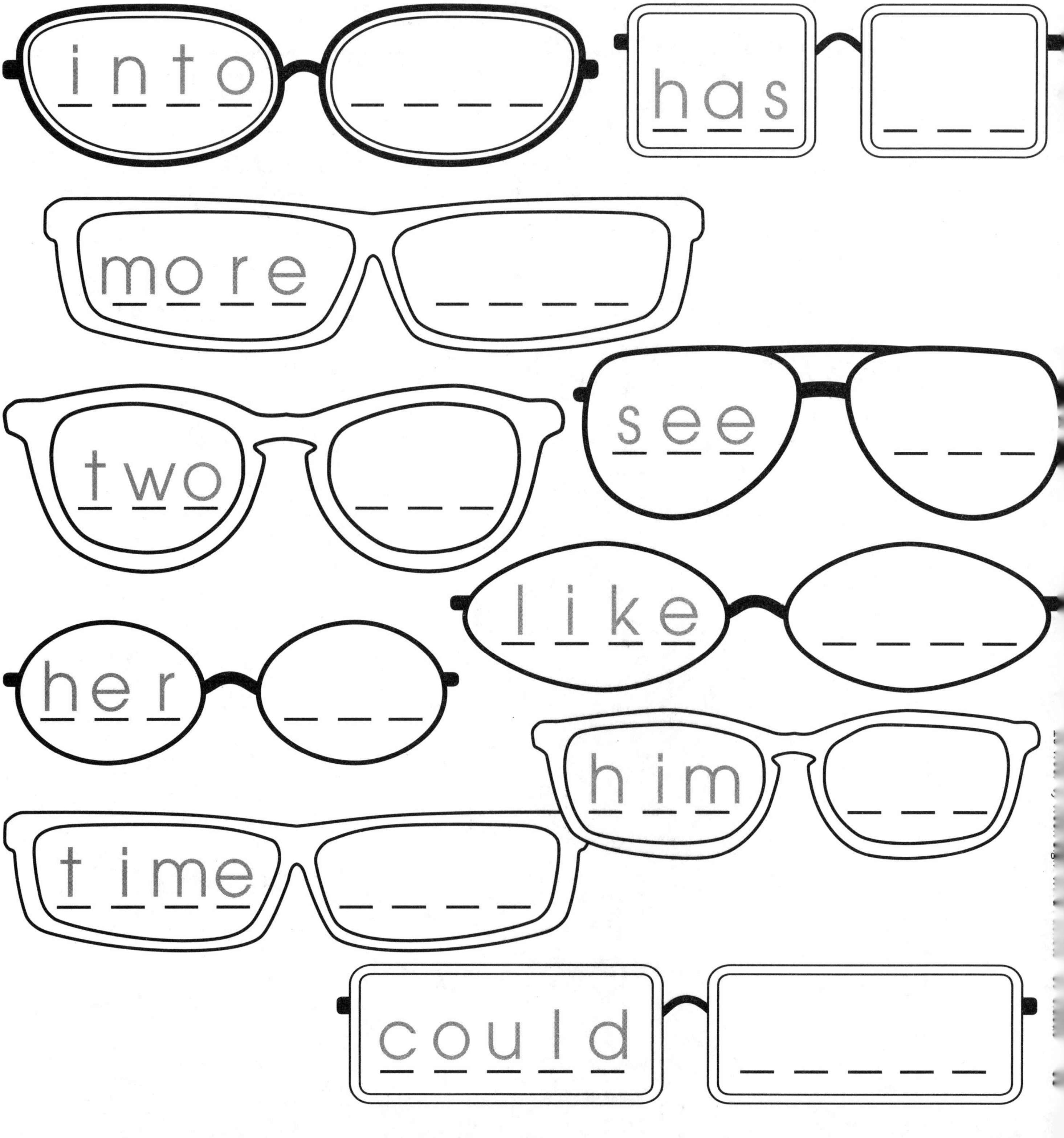

into ____

has ___

more ____

see ___

two ___

like ____

her ___

him ___

time ____

could _____

Sight Word Packet 7 Name ______________________________

One Letter at a Time

Fill in the letters one at a time to build a word pyramid. The first one has been done for you.

see

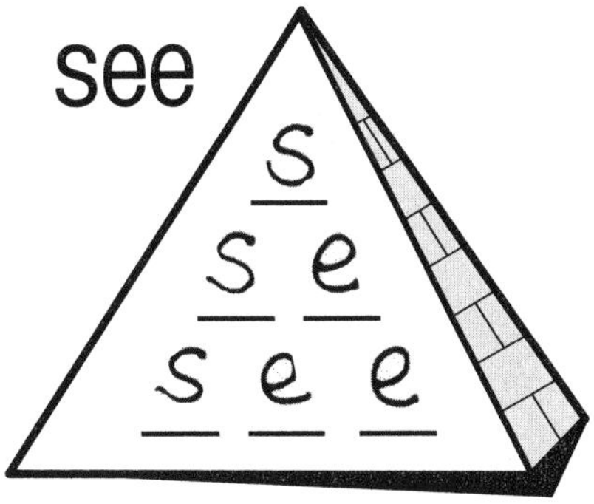

s
s e
s e e

him

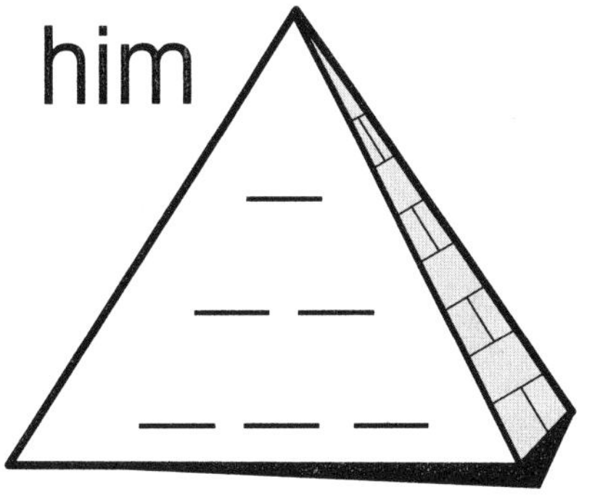

her

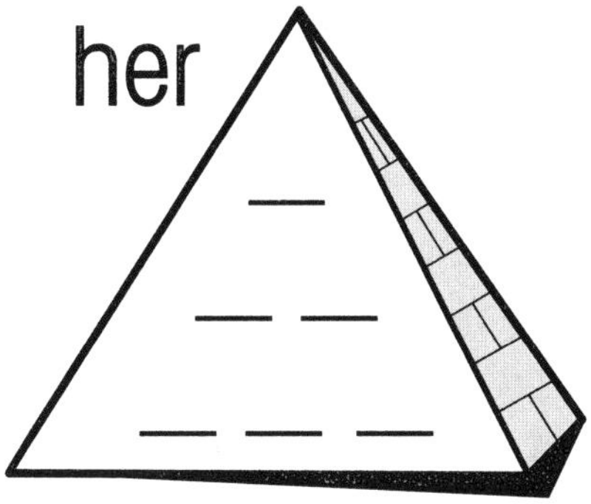

has

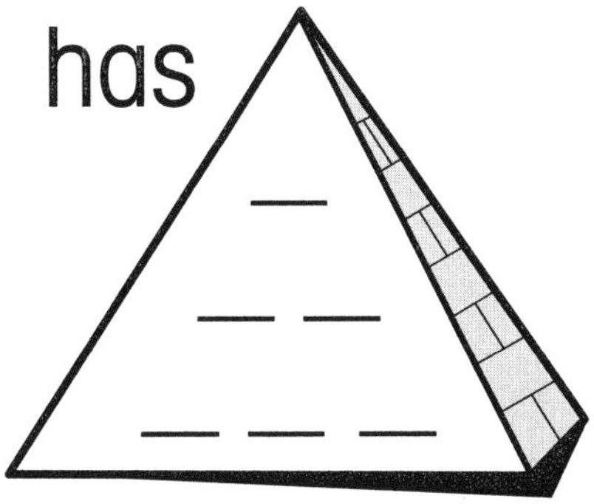

more

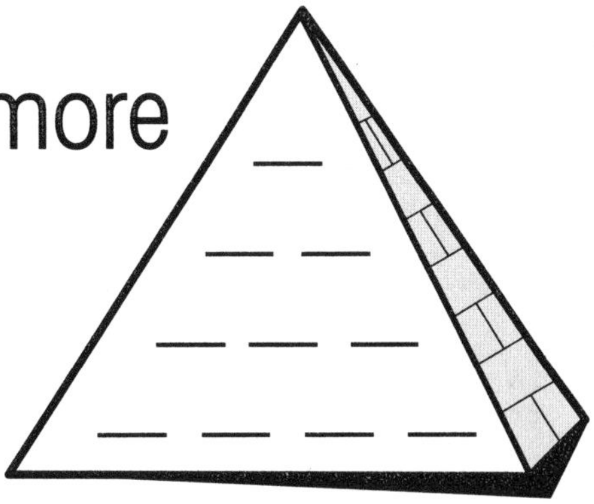

time

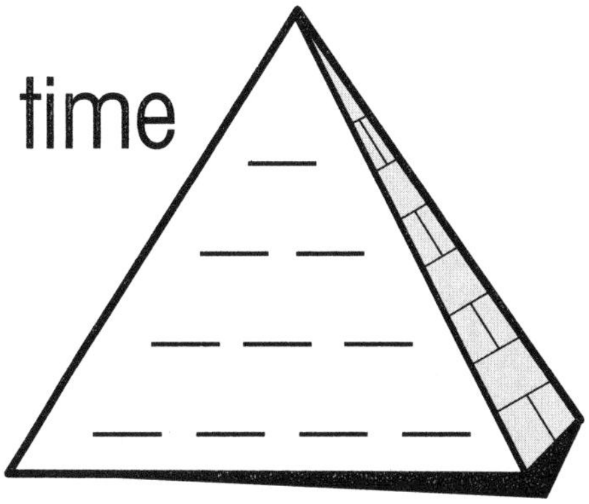

two

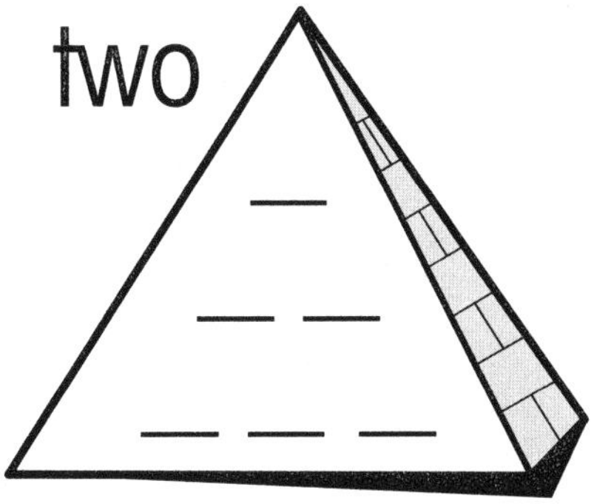

into

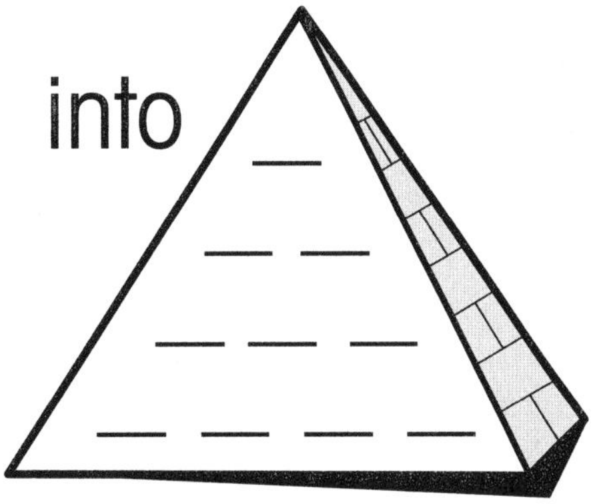

like

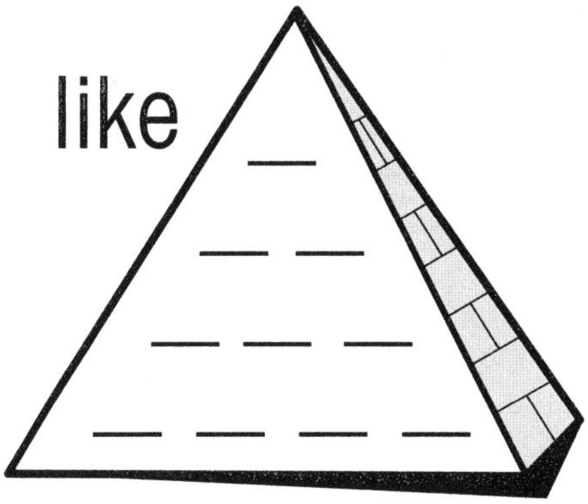

could

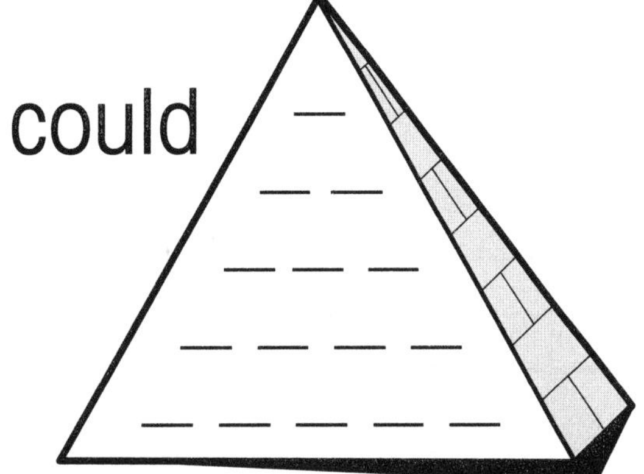

Name ____________________

Activity 3

Sorting

Towering Word Sets

Draw lines from tower to tower to match each set of words.

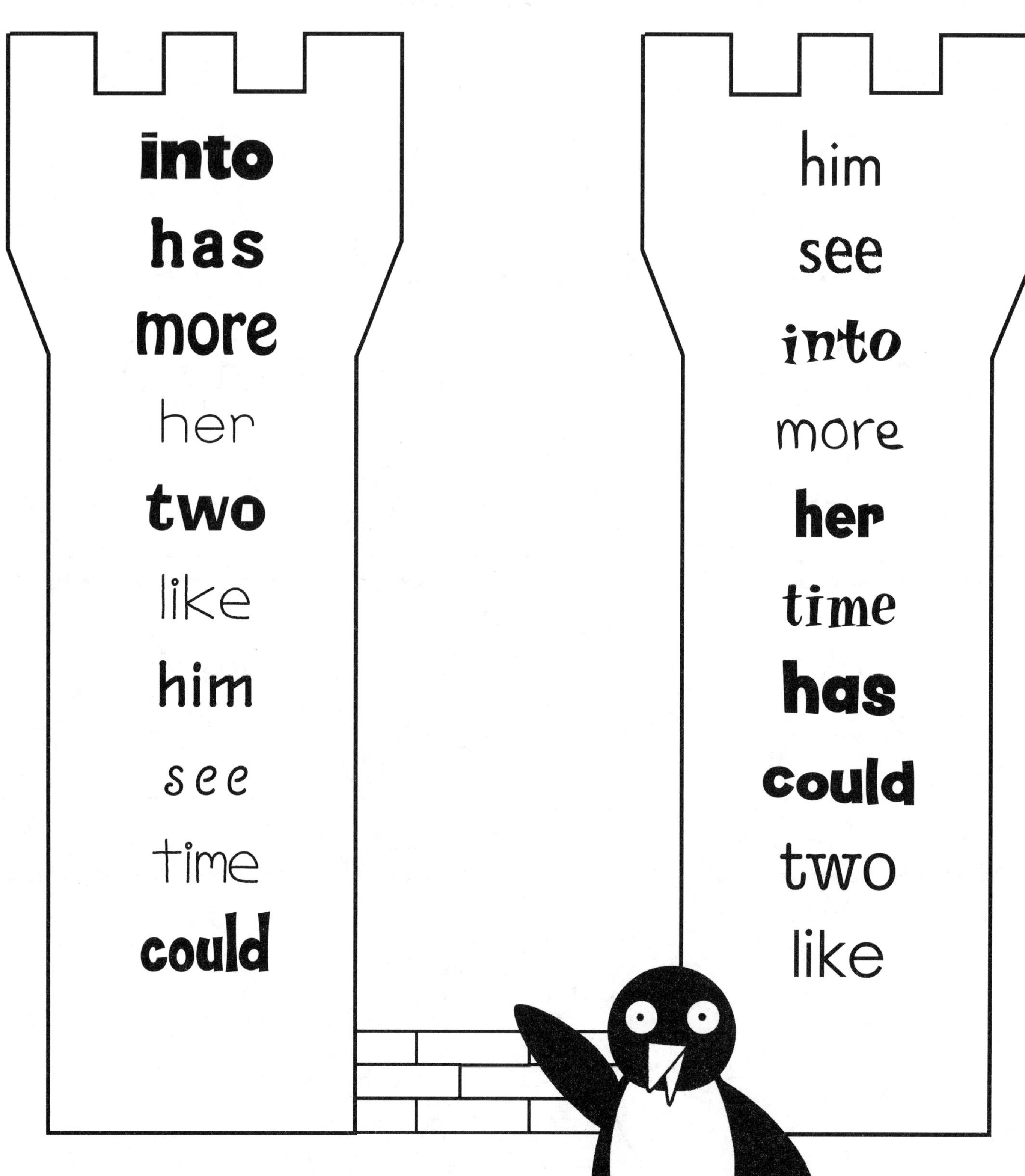

Name ______________________________

Get in Shape!

Write each word in the shape box that fits.
One has been done for you.

into	~~has~~	more	her	two
like	him	see	time	could

h a s

 Name ______________________________

Hide and Seek Word Search

Use a pencil and circle the words from the list below.
Look for words going across ⇨ and down ⇩.
The first one has been done for you.

~~INTO~~	MORE	TWO	HIM	TIME
HAS	HER	LIKE	SEE	COULD

M	O	T	W	O	M	P	H	E	R
H	A	S	X	W	O	D	P	M	T
G	A	H	G	T	R	R	T	S	I
V	L	I	K	E	E	J	O	K	M
Z	E	M	B	S	R	T	W	Z	E
T	P	K	D	S	E	E	X	V	S
U	W	D	T	S	C	O	U	L	D
V	F	Q	N	W	F	D	W	T	N
R	K	I	N	Q	D	X	L	Y	Z
N	Y	I	N	T	O	L	O	H	L

Name ______________________________

Picture It!

Read each sentence and look at the pictures. Draw a line to connect each picture to the sentence it goes with.

The two girls will go into the store.

I like this park. It has more we can do.

I can see him in the window.

What time is her birthday party?

I could play with this cat all day!

Name ______________________________

Listen to Me!

Have fun reading each word aloud to your family using the different voices. Be sure to get your paper signed and return it to school.

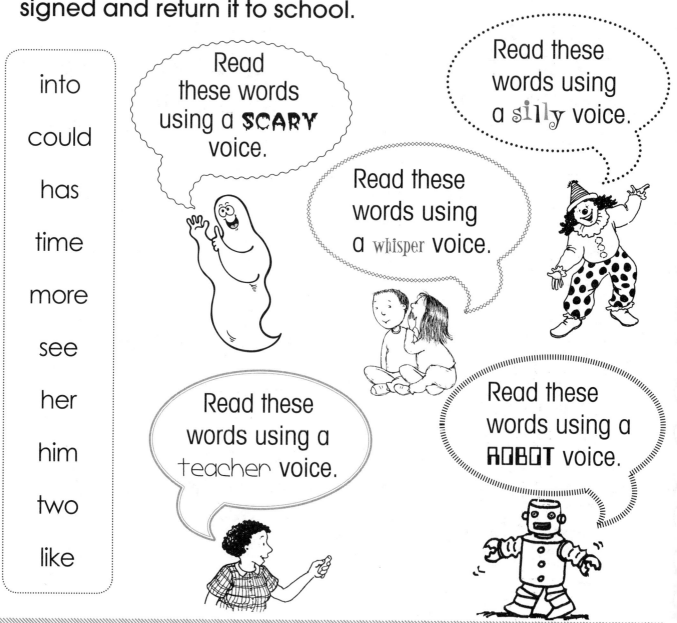

- into
- could
- has
- time
- more
- see
- her
- him
- two
- like

Read these words using a SCARY voice.

Read these words using a silly voice.

Read these words using a whisper voice.

Read these words using a teacher voice.

Read these words using a ROBOT voice.

______________________ read _____ out of 10 words quickly and accurately.

______________________________________ Parent/Guardian Signature

Name ______________________________

no	make
first	than
been	its
who	now
people	my

✔ off each activity after you complete it.

- ❑ Activity 1: **Tracing**
- ❑ Activity 2: **Building**
- ❑ Activity 3: **Sorting**
- ❑ Activity 4: **Rewriting**
- ❑ Activity 5: **Searching**
- ❑ Activity 6: **Thinking**
- ❑ Activity 7: **Practicing**

Sight Word Packet 8 Name ______________________________

Activity 1

Tracing

Take a Good Look!

Trace each sight word. Then copy it on the lines to fill in the glasses.

Sight Word Packet 8 Name ______________________

Activity 2
Building

One Letter at a Time

Fill in the letters one at a time to build a word pyramid. One has been done for you.

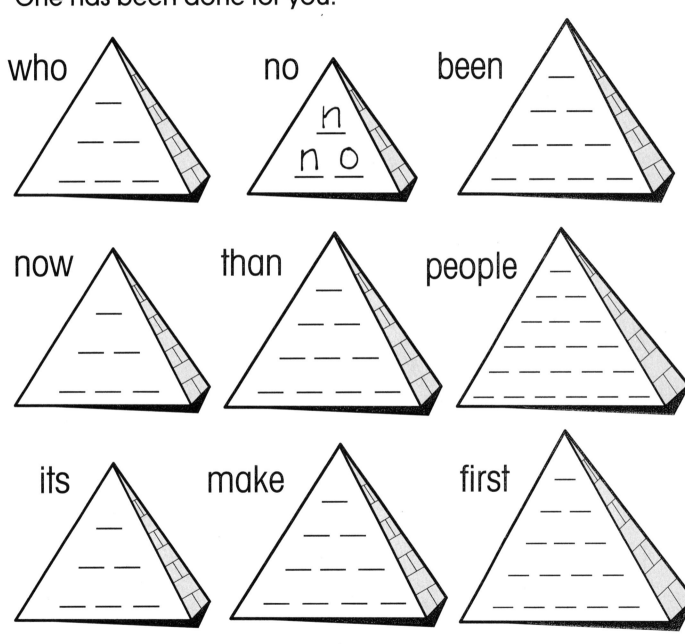

who

_

_ _

_ _ _

no

n

n o

been

_

_ _

_ _ _

_ _ _ _

now

_

_ _

_ _ _

than

_

_ _

_ _ _

_ _ _ _

people

_

_ _

_ _ _

_ _ _ _

_ _ _ _ _

_ _ _ _ _ _

its

_

_ _

_ _ _

make

_

_ _

_ _ _

_ _ _ _

first

_

_ _

_ _ _

_ _ _ _

_ _ _ _ _

my

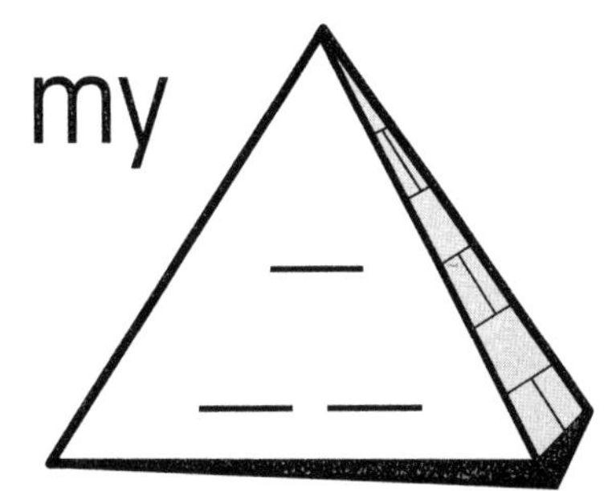

Sight Word Packet 8 Name ______________________

Activity 3

Sorting

Towering Word Sets

Draw lines from tower to tower to match each set of words.

 Name ______________________________

Get in Shape!

Write each word in the shape box that fits.
One has been done for you.

no	make	than	first	been
~~its~~	who	now	people	my

i t s

 Name ______________________________

Hide and Seek Word Search

Use a pencil and circle the words from the list below.
Look for words going across ⇨ and down ⇩.
The first one has been done for you.

~~NO~~	THAN	BEEN	WHO	PEOPLE
MAKE	FIRST	ITS	NOW	MY

```
M Y L M A K E J O Z
Q F F I R S T H A N
U N A B N F I T S D
F O V B S X L G P A
Y W M O O C B E E N
D K S W M V W H O O
S R P S X A K B P L
V Q I C L H X A L K
N Z J H U M V L E O
L I C J H O D M T R
```

 Name ____________________

Picture It!

Read each sentence and look at the pictures. Draw a line to connect each picture to the sentence it goes with.

Who finished first?

I can make a better pizza than you!

That's a big dog. This is its ball!

My Grandma asked, "How have you been?"

Mom said, "No. We can't go to the park now."

Sight Word Packet 8 Name ____________________

Activity 7

Practicing

Listen to Me!

Have fun reading each word aloud to your family using the different voices. Be sure to get your paper signed and return it to school.

no

my

make

people

than

now

first

who

been

its

Read these words using a SCARY voice.

Read these words using a silly voice.

Read these words using a whisper voice.

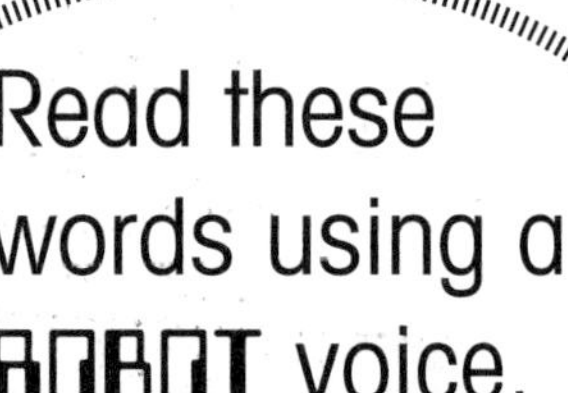

Read these words using a teacher voice.

Read these words using a ROBOT voice.

____________________ read _____ out of 10 words quickly and accurately.

____________________ Parent/Guardian Signature

Name ______________________________

Sight Word Packet 9

made did

over down

way only

find use

may water

✔ off each activity after you complete it.

- ❑ Activity 1: **Tracing**
- ❑ Activity 2: **Building**
- ❑ Activity 3: **Sorting**
- ❑ Activity 4: **Rewriting**
- ❑ Activity 5: **Searching**
- ❑ Activity 6: **Thinking**
- ❑ Activity 7: **Practicing**

Name ____________________

Activity 1
Tracing

Take a Good Look!

Trace each sight word. Then copy it on the lines to fill in the glasses.

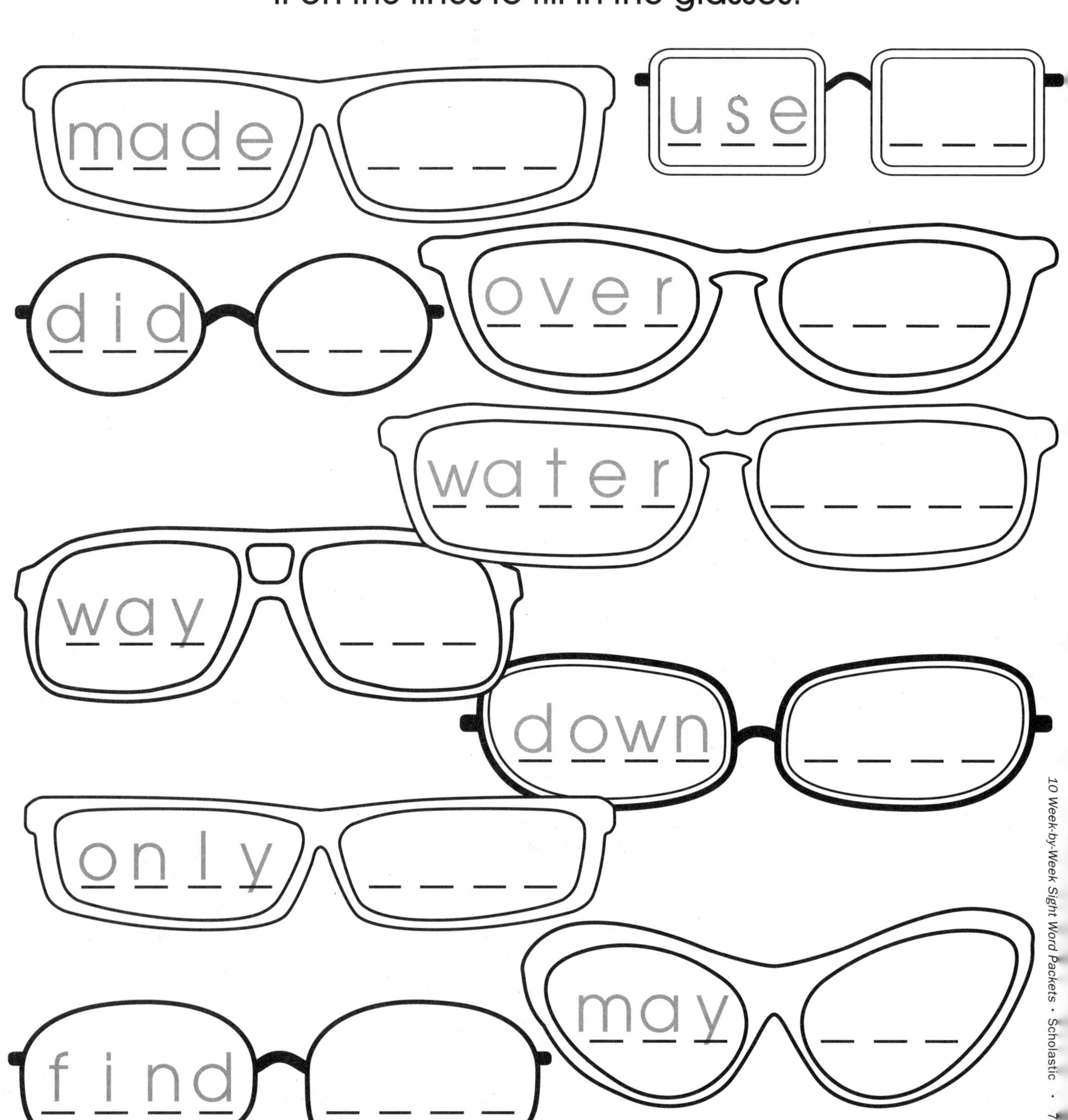

 Name ______________________

One Letter at a Time

Fill in the letters one at a time to build a word pyramid. The first one has been done for you.

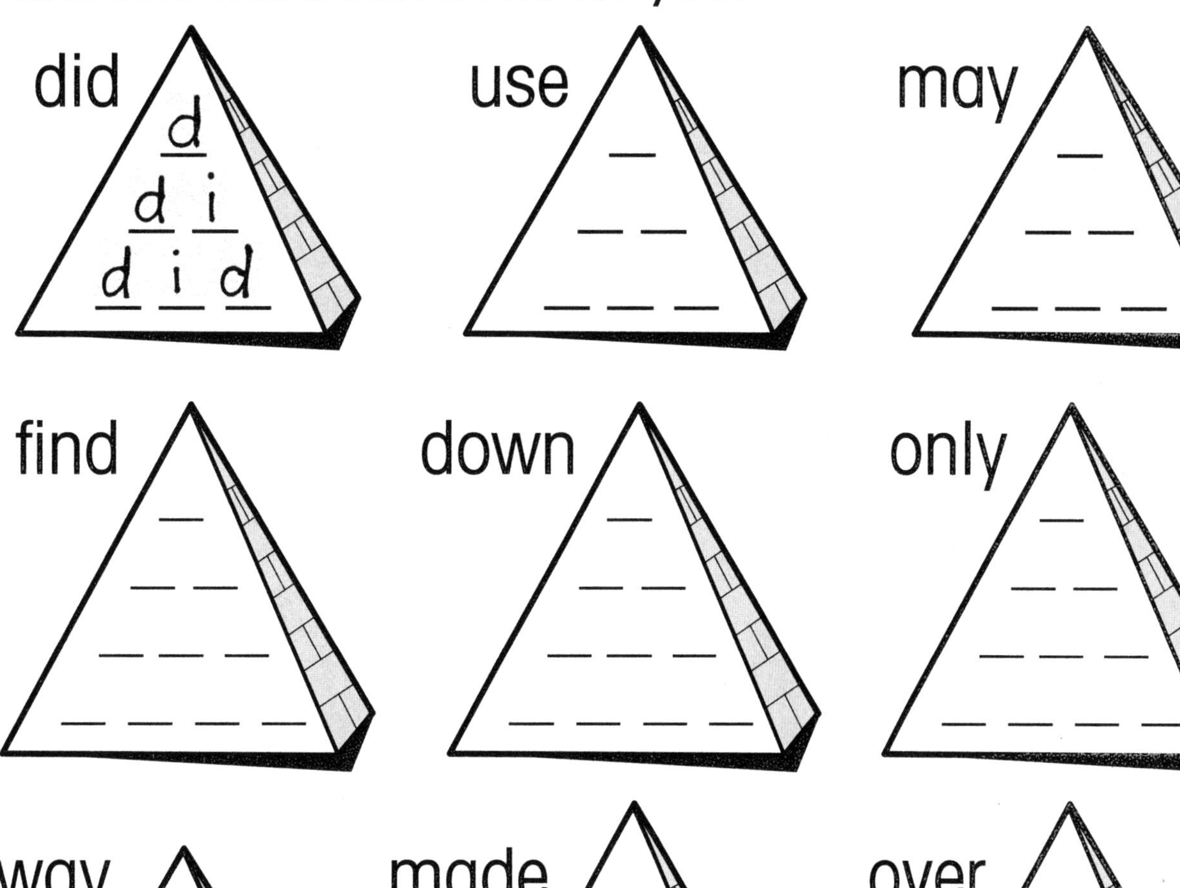

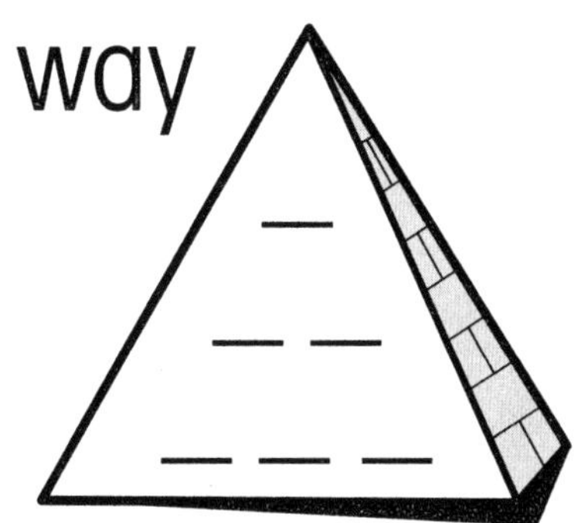

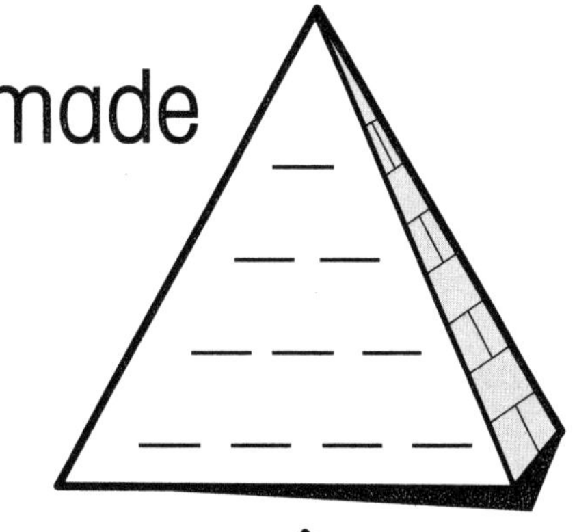

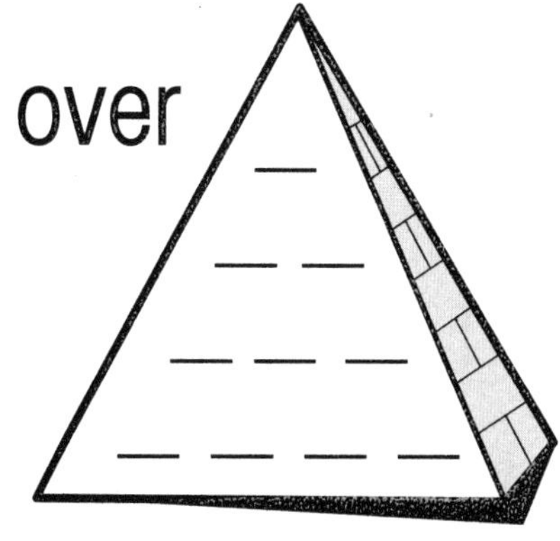

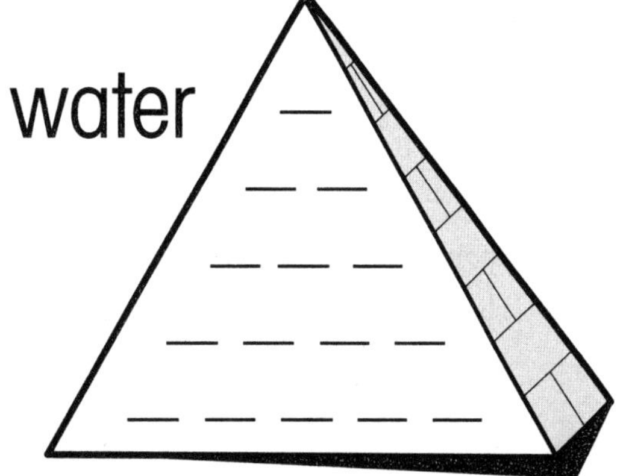

Sight Word Packet 9 Name ____________________

Activity 3
Sorting

Towering Word Sets

Draw lines from tower to tower to match each set of words.

made	water
over	only
did	over
down	find
only	did
way	down
find	way
use	made
may	use
water	may

Name ____________________

Activity 4
Rewriting

Get in Shape!

Write each word in the shape box that fits. One has been done for you.

made	over	did	down	only
~~way~~	find	use	may	water

w a y

 Name ______________________________

Hide and Seek Word Search

Use a pencil and circle the words from the list below.
Look for words going across ⇨ and down ⇩.
The first one has been done for you.

~~MADE~~	DID	ONLY	FIND	MAY
OVER	DOWN	WAY	USE	WATER

M	M	C	W	O	A	O	A	Y	F
A	A	V	A	V	N	K	V	V	I
I	Y	W	T	E	D	M	P	D	N
C	U	S	E	R	O	V	X	A	D
Y	O	S	R	B	W	T	M	D	Q
W	A	Y	W	I	N	Y	R	H	H
W	M	A	D	E	Y	W	T	E	D
D	Y	Z	A	D	Y	L	T	T	Y
I	M	L	Y	S	B	T	N	U	A
D	V	R	C	O	N	L	Y	O	L

 Name ____________________

Picture It!

Read each sentence and look at the pictures. Draw a line to connect each picture to the sentence it goes with.

We went over to the park and down the slide.

Can you find your way home on the map?

Did you use water to wash your hands?

We made only cupcakes for the party.

May I go outside and ride my bike?

Sight Word Packet 9 Name ______________________

Activity 7

Practicing

Listen to Me!

Have fun reading each word aloud to your family using the different voices. Be sure to get your paper signed and return it to school.

- made
- water
- over
- may
- did
- use
- down
- find
- only
- way

Read these words using a SCARY voice.

Read these words using a silly voice.

Read these words using a whisper voice.

Read these words using a teacher voice.

Read these words using a ROBOT voice.

______________________ read _____ out of 10 words quickly and accurately.

______________________________________ Parent/Guardian Signature

Name ______________________________

little	long
just	where
very	after
called	words
most	know

✔ off each activity after you complete it.

- ❏ Activity 1: **Tracing**
- ❏ Activity 2: **Building**
- ❏ Activity 3: **Sorting**
- ❏ Activity 4: **Rewriting**
- ❏ Activity 5: **Searching**
- ❏ Activity 6: **Thinking**
- ❏ Activity 7: **Practicing**

 Name ______________________

Take a Good Look!

Trace each sight word. Then copy it on the lines to fill in the glasses.

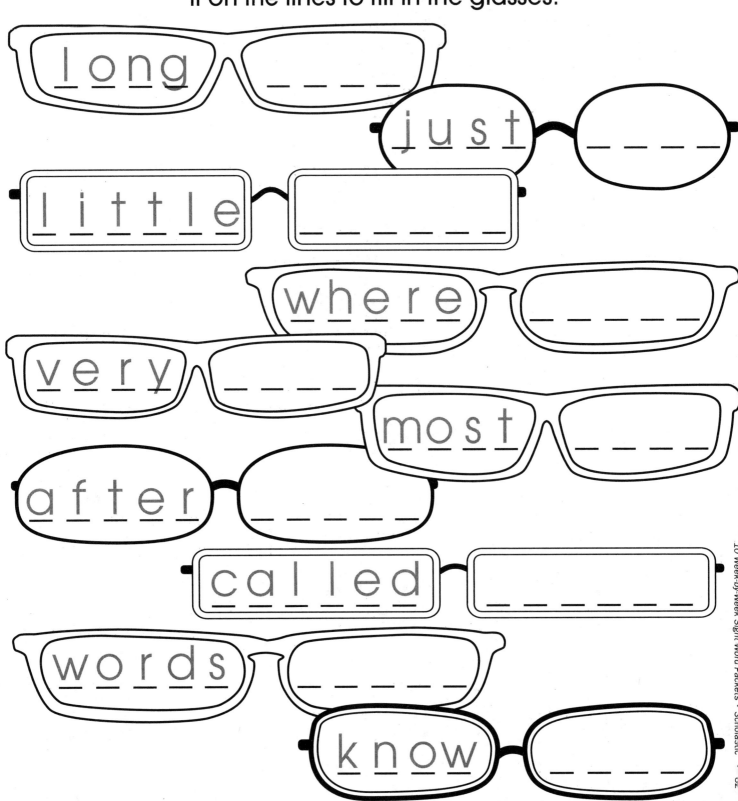

long _ _ _ _

just _ _ _ _

little _ _ _ _ _ _

where _ _ _ _ _

very _ _ _ _

most _ _ _ _

after _ _ _ _ _

called _ _ _ _ _ _

words _ _ _ _ _

know _ _ _ _

 Name ______________________

One Letter at a Time

Fill in the letters one at a time to build a word pyramid. The first one has been done for you.

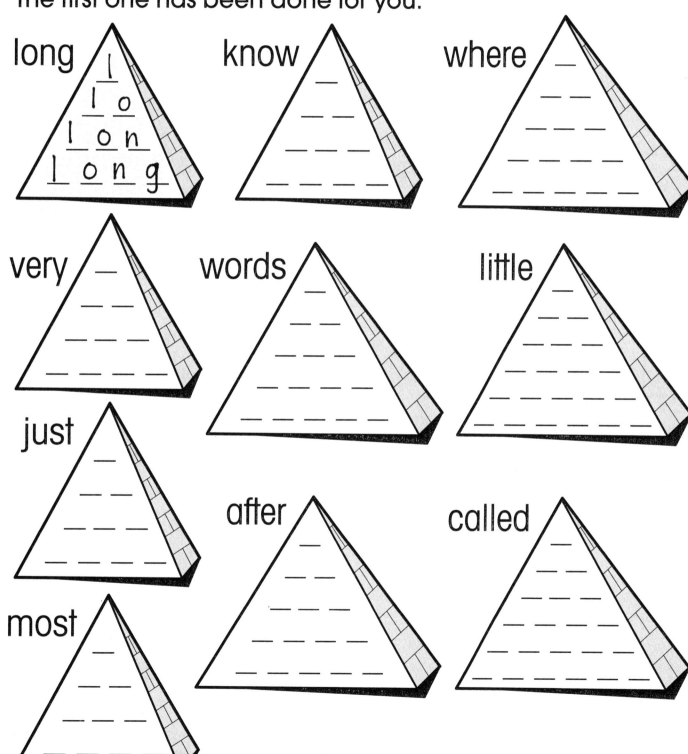

long
l
l o
l o n
l o n g

know

where

very

words

little

just

after

called

most

 Name ____________________

Towering Word Sets

Draw lines from tower to tower to match each set of words.

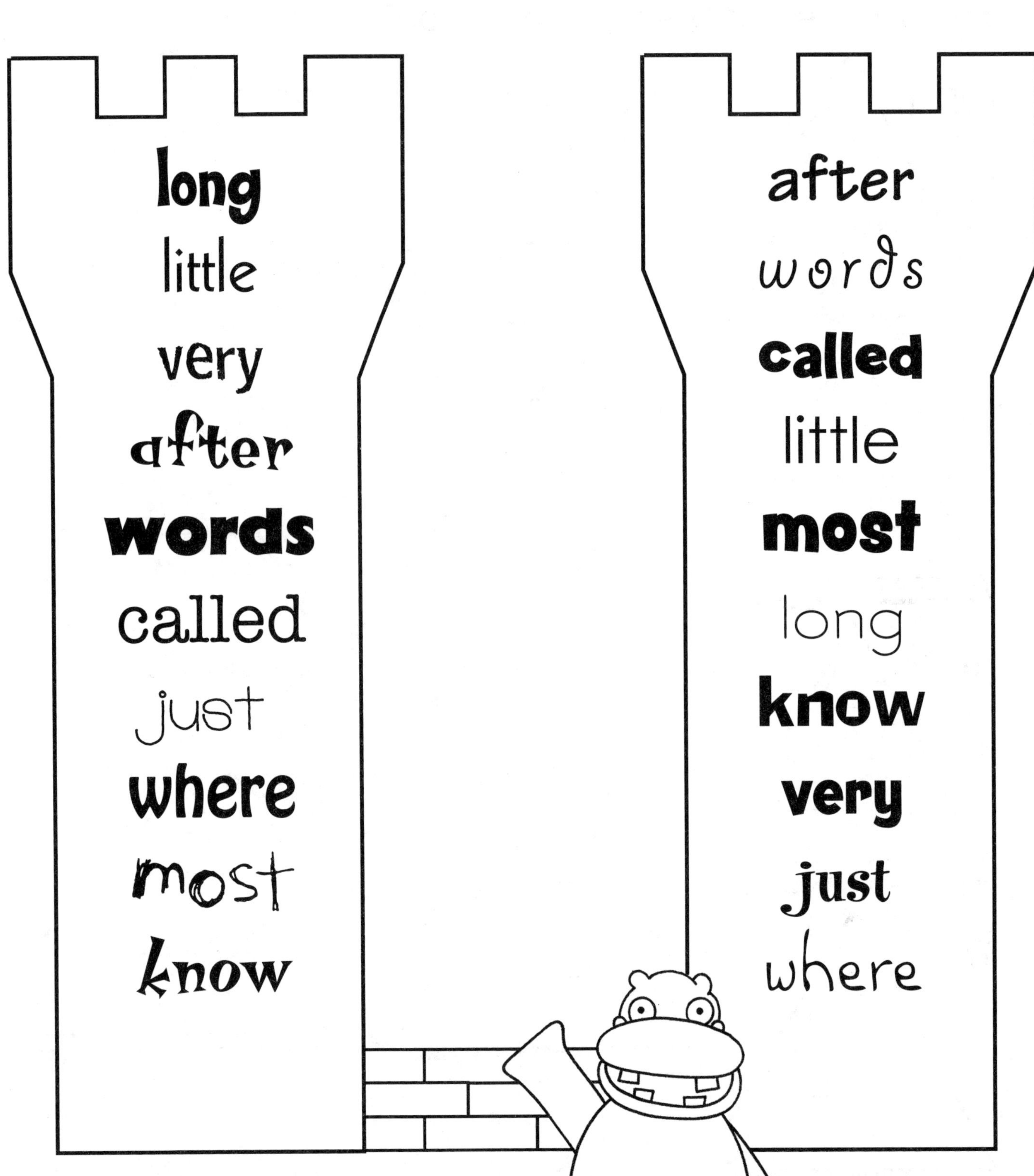

Name ______________________________

Get in Shape!

Write each word in the shape box that fits.
One has been done for you.

long	little	~~very~~	after	words
called	just	where	most	know

v e r y

Sight Word Packet 10 Name ______________________________

Activity 5

Searching

Hide and Seek Word Search

Use a pencil and circle the words from the list below.
Look for words going across ⇨ and down ⇩.
The first one has been done for you.

~~LONG~~	VERY	WORDS	JUST	MOST
LITTLE	AFTER	CALLED	WHERE	KNOW

Z D P N U O Y J W L

P M R A F T E R L V

D V E R Y Z H K I H

M O S T Y R D N T V

Q W J U S T R O T C

Q O L B M Z P W L D

L R J Z C A L L E D

O D W Z W H E R E F

N S G T L P I Y A W

G X D Z M Z U K G J

 Name ____________________

Picture It!

Read each sentence and look at the pictures. Draw a line to connect each picture to the sentence it goes with.

I know how to spell most of the words for my spelling test.

"I do not like fish. Please give me only a little bit."

I have not called grandma in a very long time.

"Excuse me. Where is the shoe store?"

We have just enough cookies.

 Name ____________________

Listen to Me!

Have fun reading each word aloud to your family using the different voices. Be sure to get your paper signed and return it to school.

long
know
little
most
very
where
after
just
words
called

Read these words using a SCARY voice.

Read these words using a silly voice.

Read these words using a whisper voice.

Read these words using a teacher voice.

Read these words using a ROBOT voice.

____________________ read _____ out of 10 words quickly and accurately.

____________________ Parent/Guardian Signature

the Sight Word Packet 1	in Sight Word Packet 1
of Sight Word Packet 1	is Sight Word Packet 1
that Sight Word Packet 1	you Sight Word Packet 1
a Sight Word Packet 1	and Sight Word Packet 1
to Sight Word Packet 1	it Sight Word Packet 1

he Sight Word Packet 2	his Sight Word Packet 2
at Sight Word Packet 2	on Sight Word Packet 2
for Sight Word Packet 2	with Sight Word Packet 2
they Sight Word Packet 2	are Sight Word Packet 2
was Sight Word Packet 2	as Sight Word Packet 2

be Sight Word Packet 3	one Sight Word Packet 3
not Sight Word Packet 3	I Sight Word Packet 3
this Sight Word Packet 3	by Sight Word Packet 3
had Sight Word Packet 3	have Sight Word Packet 3
from Sight Word Packet 3	or Sight Word Packet 3

but Sight Word Packet 4	can Sight Word Packet 4
your Sight Word Packet 4	were Sight Word Packet 4
what Sight Word Packet 4	there Sight Word Packet 4
an Sight Word Packet 4	when Sight Word Packet 4
all Sight Word Packet 4	we Sight Word Packet 4

which Sight Word Packet 5	about Sight Word Packet 5
up Sight Word Packet 5	if Sight Word Packet 5
their Sight Word Packet 5	each Sight Word Packet 5
how Sight Word Packet 5	do Sight Word Packet 5
said Sight Word Packet 5	will Sight Word Packet 5

out Sight Word Packet 6	these Sight Word Packet 6
other Sight Word Packet 6	she Sight Word Packet 6
them Sight Word Packet 6	so Sight Word Packet 6
would Sight Word Packet 6	many Sight Word Packet 6
then Sight Word Packet 6	some Sight Word Packet 6

into Sight Word Packet 7	see Sight Word Packet 7
could Sight Word Packet 7	her Sight Word Packet 7
has Sight Word Packet 7	him Sight Word Packet 7
time Sight Word Packet 7	two Sight Word Packet 7
more Sight Word Packet 7	like Sight Word Packet 7

no Sight Word Packet 8	now Sight Word Packet 8
my Sight Word Packet 8	first Sight Word Packet 8
make Sight Word Packet 8	who Sight Word Packet 8
people Sight Word Packet 8	been Sight Word Packet 8
than Sight Word Packet 8	its Sight Word Packet 8

made Sight Word Packet 9	use Sight Word Packet 9	long Sight Word Packet 10	where Sight Word Packet 10
water Sight Word Packet 9	down Sight Word Packet 9	know Sight Word Packet 10	after Sight Word Packet 10
over Sight Word Packet 9	find Sight Word Packet 9	little Sight Word Packet 10	just Sight Word Packet 10
may Sight Word Packet 9	only Sight Word Packet 9	most Sight Word Packet 10	words Sight Word Packet 10
did Sight Word Packet 9	way Sight Word Packet 9	very Sight Word Packet 10	called Sight Word Packet 10

Sight Words Reading Assessment: First 100

Student Name ________________________________

UNIT 1	UNIT 2	UNIT 3	UNIT 4	UNIT 5
Assessment Dates	Assessment Dates	Assessment Dates	Assessment Dates	Assessment Dates
1 2 3	1 2 3	1 2 3	1 2 3	1 2 3
the	he	be	but	which
of	at	not	your	up
that	for	this	what	their
a	they	had	an	how
to	was	from	all	said
in	his	one	can	about
is	on	I	were	if
you	with	by	there	each
and	are	have	when	do
it	as	or	we	will
totals	totals	totals	totals	totals

Sight Words Reading Assessment: First 100

Student Name ____

UNIT 6	UNIT 7	UNIT 8	UNIT 9	UNIT 10
Assessment Dates	Assessment Dates	Assessment Dates	Assessment Dates	Assessment Dates
1 2 3	1 2 3	1 2 3	1 2 3	1 2 3
☐☐☐ out	☐☐☐ into	☐☐☐ no	☐☐☐ made	☐☐☐ long
☐☐☐ other	☐☐☐ could	☐☐☐ my	☐☐☐ water	☐☐☐ know
☐☐☐ them	☐☐☐ has	☐☐☐ make	☐☐☐ over	☐☐☐ little
☐☐☐ would	☐☐☐ time	☐☐☐ people	☐☐☐ may	☐☐☐ most
☐☐☐ then	☐☐☐ more	☐☐☐ than	☐☐☐ did	☐☐☐ very
☐☐☐ these	☐☐☐ see	☐☐☐ now	☐☐☐ use	☐☐☐ where
☐☐☐ she	☐☐☐ her	☐☐☐ first	☐☐☐ down	☐☐☐ after
☐☐☐ so	☐☐☐ him	☐☐☐ who	☐☐☐ find	☐☐☐ just
☐☐☐ many	☐☐☐ two	☐☐☐ been	☐☐☐ only	☐☐☐ words
☐☐☐ some	☐☐☐ like	☐☐☐ its	☐☐☐ way	☐☐☐ called
____ totals	____ totals	____ totals	____ totals	____ totals

Answers

Sight Word Packet 1

Y J G S J B R A W Z
B T T H E I U C L T
C O P C O X Y D B H
M I S E S N O A V A
I S K Z M L U Z C T
E O O F G P A R O N
I K M F C O N K S X
T V S Y J D D N R I
P E C C O Z Y D Z B
D E H D M F I N D E

Sight Word Packet 2

S J Y Q Z T M X U B
R M F O R B J A R E
H H P M D F C Y A O
I Y N K X L A X S N
S W W A S I E N D R
K W I T H H R U I L
T H E Y B A B L I C
D A T H G A M E V C
H E T H R S C U B H
I H X Q V Q Y D R A

Sight Word Packet 3

B J P Y N Q L B R F
J G F R O M U R D N
I B D X T D I X T F
Q T G Z Z C C I S M
V B Y A G P Q K O B
A D C X R I J U R M
O T H I S X L Y D B
N S A H A V E G N E
E V D E R V H N G V
S T Y U M F Q J Q D

Sight Word Packet 4

R S V F H E G J S D
Q Q T A Y O H U L G
N O T Y O U R W P I
S K W Y W K B Z J D
F N E Q J S T A C S
U E R A B E H H E Z
W H E N U Q E C A N
M W H A T B R L L S
A P V L Y T E F L X
Q Z X A O F K L W E

Sight Word Packet 5

N S A I D E K X R W
W H H N C A D Y X E
H G C P A B O U T A
I U D T H E I R L C
C U P W B H F E H H
H O W S W W J U U N
S B J N I Q A W S V
T F N X L H U F C H
U A B B L X W F S T
U L J I T I R G E O

Sight Word Packet 6

Sight Word Packet 7

M O T W O M P H E R
H A S X W O D P M T
G A H G T R R T S I
V L I K E E J O K M
Z E M B S R T W Z E
T P K D S E E X V S
U W D T S C O U L D
V F Q N W F D W T N
R K I N Q D X L Y Z
N Y I N T O L O H L

Sight Word Packet 8

M Y L M A K E J O Z
Q F F I R S T H A N
U N A B N F I T S D
F O V B S X L G P A
Y W M O O C B E E N
D K S W M V W H O O
S R P S X A K B P L
V Q I C L H X A L K
N Z J H U M V L E O
L I C J H O D M T R

Sight Word Packet 9

M M C W O A O A Y F
A A V A V N K V V I
I Y W T E D M P D N
C U S E R O V X A D
Y O S R B W T M D Q
W A Y W I N Y R H H
W M A D E Y W T E D
D Y Z A D Y L T T Y
I M L Y S B T N U A
D V R C O N L Y O L

Sight Word Packet 10

Z D P N U O Y J W L
P M R A F T E R L V
D V E R Y Z H K I H
M O S T Y R D N T V
Q W J U S T R O T C
Q O L B M Z P W L D
L R J Z C A L L E D
O D W Z W H E R E F
N S G T L P I Y A W
G X D Z M Z U K G J